CHALKBOARD CHAMPIONS

Twelve Remarkable Teachers Who Educated America's Disenfranchised Students

Terry Lee Marzell

Chalkboard Champions: Twelve Remarkable Teachers Who Educated America's Disenfranchised Students

Published by Wheatmark®
1760 East River Road, Suite 145,
Tucson, Arizona 85718 U.S.A.
www.wheatmark.com

ISBN: 978-1-60494-810-3 (paperback)
ISBN: 978-1-60494-834-9 (ebook)
LCCN: 2012939586

This book is dedicated to my loving husband,
Hal Marzell, who every day teaches me how to be
a better person, and to my mother, Jana Bradberry,
who was my first teacher, and to all of the remarkable
teachers with whom I work.

TABLE OF CONTENTS

PREFACE

In January 2010, my husband, Hal, and I traveled halfway across the country to spend an extended weekend in Little Rock, Arkansas. Admittedly, Little Rock is not high on the list of popular tourist destinations, but we were on a mission. Our purpose was to visit the Clinton Presidential Library and Museum. We like to explore presidential libraries, and a visit to each existing institution is one of the items on our bucket list. While we were in Little Rock, we took the opportunity to visit a small, inconspicuous museum located across the street from the city's Central High School. The museum is dedicated to a group of African American students, known as the Little Rock Nine, and the historic events that surrounded their attempt to challenge the Jim Crow South by integrating the school. The museum's exhibits were well prepared, visually appealing, and very informative, an impressive feat for such a small enterprise. As I perused the exhibits, I learned much about the accomplishments of this group of courageous individuals and their role in the civil rights movement.

I learned that on May 17, 1954, the US Supreme Court issued its landmark decision, *Brown v. Board of Education*, which declared segregated schools unconstitutional. I discovered that Virgil Blossom, then superintendent of schools in Little Rock, had prepared a plan for integration with the goal of implementation by September 1957. The plan generated an intensely hostile response from Little Rock's staunch segregationists, who, with the support of Arkansas Governor Orval Faubus and the backing of the Arkansas National Guard, effectively blocked the entrance of the nine African American students who had been selected to integrate the high school. President Dwight Eisenhower attempted to persuade Governor Faubus to abide by the law. When Faubus stubbornly refused, the president mobilized the army's 101st US Airborne Division, federalized the Arkansas National Guard, and charged the troops with the duty of protecting the lives of the young students and enforcing the Supreme Court's ruling. Every school day that year, the Little Rock Nine braved angry mobs spewing hostilities, racial epithets, and threats to their lives simply for seeking the right to enter their school.

The educator in me wondered what Central High's teachers were doing during these historic events. Were they supporting the students openly, or secretly, if necessary, or were they contributing to the racist chaos? What can a teacher do, what is a teacher expected to do, in highly charged periods of social change, political upheaval, or times of war?

Curiosity launched me onto a path of intellectual inquiry which led me to discover many accounts of remarkable teachers who worked with disenfranchised groups of students throughout American history. In this volume you will find the extraordinary stories of twelve of them, but there are many more remarkable stories that could be told.

In selecting the teachers who are presented here, I employed a distinct set of criteria. I looked for individuals who had completed a teacher certification course or had at least received some training in educational pedagogy. I searched for individuals who could identify teaching as their primary life profession, and I wanted to find teachers who spent a significant portion of their teaching career at the elementary or secondary level. Although many of the selected teachers can boast major accomplishments outside of their classroom teaching assignments, most spent a number of years in the classroom, and many of their achievements are related to or within the educational sphere. Most importantly, I looked for teachers who were working with disenfranchised groups of students, including Native Americans, African Americans, Hispanic Americans, immigrants, orphans, the handicapped, children from impoverished families, internees, or inner-city youths. Finally, I looked for stories that I judged to be intriguing, uplifting, and inspirational, not only for the reader who is an educator, but also for the general-interest reader.

Although each individual presented in this volume is an extraordinary educator, each one is also a real person, with strengths and weaknesses just like any other human being. As energetic, ambitious, and dynamic intellectuals, each one possessed a personality that was complex and multifaceted. Their foibles and idiosyncrasies, I hope, will be forgiven when balanced with their remarkable and heroic successes.

My desire is that these stories will fill the beginning teacher with enthusiasm, reignite the joy of the classroom experience in the veteran teacher, and generate an admiration for the profession in the general reader. Enjoy!

To me the sole hope of human salvation lies in teaching.
GEORGE BERNARD SHAW

Charlotte Forten Grimke educated newly-freed slaves in an Emancipation School in Port Royal, South Carolina, during the Civil War. Photo undated.

1

CHARLOTTE FORTEN GRIMKE
She Taught Emancipated Slaves

Education makes people easy to lead, but difficult to drive;
easy to govern, but impossible to enslave.
HENRY PETER BROUGHAM

It was January 1, 1863, and a hint of Christmas excitement still hung in the air. Charlotte Forten, her fellow missionaries, and her abolitionist companions waited with eager anticipation in a shady grove of gnarled and ancient live oaks, which were draped decoratively with garlands of Spanish moss. Among those assembled were a group of Union army officers and their regiment of African American soldiers, all impressively decked out in handsome blue coats and scarlet slacks, each one carrying a brightly polished bayonet. An exultant crowd of escaped slaves—some say five thousand of them—had also amassed. The multitude had gathered together at this place to mark a historic event of monumental importance: the official reading of the Emancipation Proclamation. First were the prayers, then the speeches, the songs, the presentation of the flags, and finally, the reading of the Proclamation by a local minister. Forever after, the particular tree under which that minister stood would be known as the Proclamation Tree. At the conclusion of the reading, Charlotte was astonished when the jubilant throng burst out in a spontaneous rendition of "My Country 'Tis of Thee." "It was a touching and beautiful incident, and sent a thrill through all our hearts," she recorded in her diary that day. "Nothing c'ld have been better, more perfect" (Grimke 1988, 430).

Charlotte had journeyed to this place, Port Royal in the Sea Islands of Beaufort County, South Carolina, less than three months earlier. She had accepted a teaching position on nearby St. Helena Island. Her students were the children of plantation slaves abandoned by their white owners as they fled from advancing Union troops following the Northern victory at the Battle of Port Royal on November 7, 1861. Once the area had been liberated from Confederate control, hundreds of escaped slaves from other areas throughout the South also sought refuge in the Sea Islands. It quickly became obvious that the newly freed men, women, and children would need training on how to live independently and self-sufficiently, and they would also need some basic literacy skills. The US government, supported by donations from various aid societies, missionary groups, and churches, hastily established an emancipation school in the islands and recruited a staff of qualified teachers, including Charlotte Forten, from the North. Union troops protected the area, but the war was not yet won, so traveling to this region was a daring move for any woman, especially for a woman who also happened to be a free black.

Charlotte was well aware that the African Americans living in Beaufort County and throughout the South had long been denied opportunities for education. In the early 1800s, many southern states passed laws that made it illegal for slaves to learn how to read and write. Slave owners understood that educated slaves could be more difficult to control, so anyone caught teaching African Americans could be heavily fined or imprisoned. Slaves who knew how to read and write kept their skills a secret from their masters because if their plantation owners discovered they were literate, they could be severely punished. Charlotte had never suffered the indignities of slavery, nor had she ever been denied the opportunities for a quality education, but her heart went out to those who were not as fortunate as herself. She had always believed strongly that education would bring equality to African Americans, so in 1862, when the call went out for teachers to help educate the children of escaped and liberated slaves, she became one of the first to volunteer.

Charlotte Louise Bridges Forten was born on August 17, 1837, in Philadelphia, Pennsylvania. Although African American, she was born into freedom, affluence, and privilege. Her family history is distinguished and impressive. During the Revolutionary War, her paternal grandfather, James Forten, had served as a drummer, powder boy, and assistant gunner aboard the Continental army's ship *Royal Louis*. Captured by the British, he was held as a prisoner of war for seven long months. James was freed from captivity when he was traded for a British prisoner. After the war, James became apprenticed to Robert Bridges, a successful Philadelphia sailmaker. James was industrious and ambitious. In time, he bought the company from his employer. His profits soared when he designed and patented a new sail that made it easier to steer ships. But James was also a humanitarian, using his wealth to purchase the freedom of several slaves and assisting others to liberty by turning his home into a way station for the Underground Railroad (Bolden 1998, 30–31).

Charlotte's parents, aristocratic and altruistic, were equally admirable, working tirelessly toward social causes, particularly the abolition of slavery. Her father, Robert Bridges Forten, was a member of the Philadelphia Young Men's Anti-Slavery Society, and he was also a notable mathematician, public speaker, and poet. Her mother, Mary Virginia Woods Forten, a spirited and progressive woman, was a founding member of the Philadelphia Female Anti-Slavery Society. Mary was described by those who knew her as a gentle, loving, intelligent woman, but sadly she passed away when her little Charlotte was only three years old. Throughout her childhood, Charlotte spent much of her time with her grandfather James and doting aunts and uncles from both sides of her family. Despite this devotion, Charlotte often felt alone and unloved. She grieved over the loss of her mother deeply. Although she loved her father dearly, he was a cold, distant man, and their relationship was never a close one (Burchard 1995, 11). When Charlotte was eight, her father remarried and started a new family with his second wife.

As a young child, Charlotte was educated at home with private tutors, but when she turned sixteen, she was sent to school in Salem, Massachusetts. Charlotte's father chose this seaport city of about fifteen thousand residents because of its reputation for tolerance, its integrated schools, and its international character. Salem merchants interacted with businessmen from every corner of the globe, and it was not unusual to encounter traders from China, India, the Middle East, and Africa on the city's streets. Additionally, a number of successful and civic-minded African Americans had settled in Salem. It was decided that Charlotte would journey to Massachusetts to live in the home of family friends, Charles Lenox Remond and his wife, Amy Matilda. Like the Fortens, the Remonds were highly respected members of the New England black elite. They were educated, aristocratic, and philanthropic. And like the Fortens, they were actively committed to the antislavery movement.

In Salem, Charlotte was enrolled in Higginson Grammar School, a private academy for young women, to pursue her secondary education. Although the school embraced a policy of integration, Charlotte was the only African American out of the two hundred students who attended. Her classmates were pleasant and courteous but also rather aloof, and Charlotte found it difficult to forge any strong or lasting friendships with them. Instead, Charlotte formed attachments to her hostess, Amy Matilda Remond, who became like a second mother to her; to her teachers; and to her school principal, Mary Shepard, with whom she maintained a lifelong friendship. The curriculum at the Higginson academy placed an emphasis on critical thinking, history, geography, drawing, and cartography. Charlotte was an eager student, applying herself diligently to her coursework. She also devoted herself to keeping a daily diary, reading the classics, learning foreign languages, writing poetry, practicing music lessons, and sewing.

Although Charlotte was born and raised in Philadelphia, she swiftly learned to appreciate Salem. A nature lover, she frequently delighted in an afternoon stroll by the Massachusetts seashore. "I shall never forget my emotions on first beholding the glorious ocean," she recorded in her diary one July day. "I stood on the shore, listening to the wild sounds of the waves. They were of the richest emerald as they rose in grandeur, then suddenly falling, broke into foam white as the drifting snow. Many mingled feelings rose to my mind. But above all others was that of perfect happiness" (Grimke 1988, 88). Sometimes she drove a carriage along the shore, rode horseback through the nearby inland valleys, and on at least one memorable occasion, donned "bloomers" to climb the cherry trees to pick some fruit.

When Charlotte completed her studies at Higginson the following year, her father made it clear that he expected her to return home to Philadelphia, find a suitable husband, and marry. Because of economic factors, his fortunes were in decline, and after all, he did have other children who needed to be educated. Charlotte had other plans for her future, however. She decided to seek training in a profession so she could make her own way in the world. Against her father's wishes, she enrolled in postsecondary courses at Salem Normal School, an institution now known as Salem State University. In the nineteenth century, a normal school provided high school graduates with training to become teachers, offering courses in subjects that future educators would be expected to teach and training on how to prepare lessons and deliver instruction. Charlotte studied both literature and teaching, and eighteen months later, in 1856, she became the first African American to graduate from Salem Normal.

Immediately after her graduation, she was offered a position at Epes Grammar School, becoming the first African American teacher hired to teach white students in a Salem public school. The job offer came at an opportune time, for by then Charlotte's father had become financially unable to support her education, and Charlotte had been forced to accept personal loans to complete her teacher training courses. While employed at Epes, Charlotte was well liked by her students and highly respected by her colleagues.

It was during her years in Salem that Charlotte, still a teenager, began to exhibit signs of failing health. She referred to her condition as "lung fever," but her malady was unquestionably a form of tuberculosis. The dreaded disease was widespread in the 1800s, and typically the diagnosis was as good as a death sentence. More than half of those afflicted succumbed within five years. Charlotte's case was not so deleterious, but her symptoms—fever, night sweats, chest pain, chronic cough, fatigue—grew steadily worse. At the end of her second year of teaching, she was forced to leave her position at Epes Grammar School and return home to Philadelphia for treatment and recuperation. Although Charlotte lived to the age of seventy-seven, her health was fragile for the rest of her life, and she was often stricken by debilitating relapses.

After Charlotte recovered from her first serious bout with tuberculosis, she returned to Salem, a city she had come to regard as a second home, to teach at her former alma mater, Higginson School. Before long, a relapse sent her back to Philadelphia. The next four years would see repeated instances where Charlotte would recover enough to accept a teaching position, only to be followed by a setback that would force her to her sickbed; one two-year-long attack very nearly brought her to the grave. By the summer of 1862, however, she appeared to be past the worst of it at last.

It was at this time that, painfully aware of her own mortality and eager to accomplish something important with her life before it was too late, Charlotte applied for a teaching position with the Port Royal Relief Association. The organization was seeking teachers to staff an emancipation school for escaped slaves, newly established in South Carolina. It seems natural that Charlotte, a young lady who had been surrounded all her life by civil rights activists and abolitionists, would devote her energy and talent to such a cause. So it was that on October 22, 1862, Charlotte set sail on the steamship *United States* bound for St. Helena Island, Port Royal, South Carolina. Charlotte, slender and graceful, sensitive and shy, intellectual and religious, was only twenty-five years old.

Four days later, the *United States* steamed into Port Royal Sound, and Charlotte got her first look at the Sea Islands, where she would live and teach for the next two years. Sandy beaches dotted by palmetto trees formed the coastline of the southern lowlands of the Beaufort County waterfront. This topography differed greatly from the jagged, rocky seascape of New England so familiar to Charlotte. The island of St. Helena was primarily a salty marshland; it was hot, muggy, inundated by fleas and mosquitoes, and accessible to the mainland only by ferryboat. This was not an ideal environment for a young woman with a history of poor health.

Charlotte spent her first week on St. Helena Island at The Oaks, an abandoned plantation house that became the headquarters of the Port Royal Relief Association. The elegant living room of The Oaks had served as the first classroom for the newly established emancipation school, but the liberated islanders were eager to become educated, and enrollment grew rapidly. Before long, 140 excited young students—and adults—presented themselves. To accommodate the numbers, the school was moved to a nearby Baptist church, a stately two-storied red brick structure built in the Federal style. When the recently arrived Charlotte toured the new schoolhouse, christened Penn School in honor of the Quaker activist William Penn, she found the one-room interior was comfortable and pleasing. It featured a brightly lit, high-ceilinged space graced by carved wooden pews, vertical windows, tall Greek columns, a raised platform situated at the front, and a balcony on either side.

"We went into the school, and heard the children read and spell," Charlotte recorded in her diary that day. "The teachers tell us that they have made great improvement in a very short time, and I noticed with pleasure how bright, how eager to learn many of them seem." Once Charlotte met her new students, she truly understood her mission. "Dear children, born in slavery, but free at last!" she wrote. "May God preserve to you all the blessings of freedom, and may you be in every possible way fitted to enjoy them. My heart goes out to you. I shall be glad to do all that I can to help you" (Grimke 1988, 391).

As an experienced teacher, Charlotte created lessons that included basic literacy skills such as reading, writing, spelling, mathematics, and history, but she quickly realized that although the former slaves were happy and celebrated their freedom, they needed training and support far beyond the traditional curriculum. They had painfully little in the way of food or clothing, they were living in dilapidated shanties that offered very little protection from the weather, and illness and disease were widespread. These resilient people worked together admirably to share their meager resources, but they desperately needed to start cultivating their own food, making their own clothes, and constructing better shelters. Additionally, as native speakers of Gullah, a Creole language with origins in the Sierra Leone region of West Africa, many of the island inhabitants needed to learn English. Charlotte found it easy, though, to dedicate herself to helping these people after she saw how determined they were to improve their own circumstances.

One of the ways Charlotte adapted her teaching methods to meet the needs of her students was to include stories about black heroes, like Toussaint L'Ouverture, the leader of the Haitian Revolution. Her efforts were well received. In her diary she wrote, "Talked to the children a little while to-day about the noble Toussaint. They listened very attentively. It is well that they should know what one of their own color could do for his race. I long to inspire them with courage and ambition (of a noble sort), and high purpose" (Grimke 1988, 397).

The adults were as eager to learn as the children. Charlotte's classroom was open to all. Among her students, Charlotte described a mother who would appear at the school every day carrying her nursing infant in her arms, and a grandmother in her sixties who attended regularly with both her adult children and her young grandchildren, taking a seat right beside the little ones. Over time, the Port Royal experiment organized adult courses to include training in agricultural sciences, carpentry, blacksmithing, and shoemaking for the men, and instruction in the domestic and needle arts for the women.

Charlotte's classroom in the red brick building, though generally comfortable, did possess some disadvantages. "In the church, we had of course but one room in which to hear all the children; and to make one's self heard, when there were often as many as a hundred and forty reciting at once, it was necessary to tax the lungs very severely," she observed in "Life on the Sea Islands" (Grimke 1864, Part I, 592). And the change of season presented an additional problem. Charlotte had expected milder winters in the South, but she found that a South Carolina winter was just as cold as those she experienced in New England. The building was damp and cold, and because there was no chimney, it was impossible to light a warming fire. By the end of the season a stove had arrived, but because it offered no ventilation, everyone choked on the smoke, and soon they had to give it up. Finding the temperature warmer outside, Charlotte moved her students outdoors. "Our school room was a pleasant one," she recalled, "... for ceiling the blue sky above, for walls, the grand old oaks with their beautiful moss-drapery—but the dampness of the ground made it unsafe for us to continue this experiment" (Grimke 1864, Part II, 670).

One of the highlights of Charlotte's sojourn in South Carolina occurred on January 31, 1863, the day she met Harriet Tubman, the legendary conductor on the Underground Railroad. Before the outbreak of the Civil War, Harriet had escaped from her slave master and fled to freedom in the North. Over the next dozen years, despite a hefty bounty on her head, Harriet risked capture and severe punishment when she returned to the South thirteen times to shepherd more than three hundred escaped slaves to freedom in Canada. A fearless and fiercely determined woman, Harriet sometimes pulled a loaded pistol on the escaped slaves if they lost their courage and threatened to turn back. During the Civil War, Harriet served the Union army as a spy, scout, nurse, and cook. "She is a wonderful woman—a real heroine," Charlotte declared in her diary that day. "My own eyes were full as I listened to her—the heroic woman! A reward of $10,000 was offered for her by the Southerners, and her friends deemed it best that she sh'ld, for a time find refuge in (Canada). And she did so, but only for a short time. She came back and was soon at the good brave work again ... I am glad I saw her—*very* glad" (Grimke 1988, 442).

Meanwhile, the War Between the States rampaged. Penn School was behind the front lines, but despite the visible presence and protection of the Union army, the dangers of war were not completely absent and at times came perilously close. The Fifty-Fourth Massachusetts Volunteer Infantry, a black regiment composed of freed slaves and commanded by Charlotte's close friend Colonel Robert Gould Shaw, engaged in battle against Confederate forces at Fort Wagner on nearby Morris Island on July 18, 1863. The regiment suffered severe casualties, more than 50 percent, and, to Charlotte's great grief, Colonel Shaw was among the slain. The wounded were carried to Port Royal for medical treatment, and word was sent to St. Helena Island that nurses and volunteers were desperately needed at the hospital facilities on the Beaufort County waterfront. Hearing this, Charlotte left her students under the supervision of a fellow teacher, raced down to the dock, and jumped aboard the Port Royal ferry that would carry her to where the wounded lay. At the hospital, she worked feverishly for several days, mending uniforms, changing bandages, distributing medicines, and writing letters home for injured soldiers (Burchard 1995, 90–91). By the end of the week, Charlotte had suffered yet another relapse of lung fever, and by the end of July, she was forced to return to Philadelphia.

Three months later, in October 1863, Charlotte returned to St. Helena Island to resume her post at the emancipation school she loved so much. She was touched by the warm welcome she received from the island residents, who held the teacher in high regard. A short while later, in May 1864, Charlotte was stunned to learn that her father, Robert Bridges Forten, had enlisted as a private in a Pennsylvania regiment of the Union army. He was later promoted to sergeant major, but after only two short months, he was stricken with typhoid fever and died. Broken-hearted over the deaths of so many she knew and loved, and her teaching assignment concluded, Charlotte decided to leave Port Royal for the last time. She returned to Philadelphia where she busied herself by writing an account of her experiences in the Port Royal experiment. Her essays, "Life on the Sea Islands, Part I and Part II," were published later that year in *Atlantic Monthly*.

When General Robert E. Lee surrendered at Appomattox Courthouse in Appomattox County, Virginia, on April 9, 1865, the Civil War was finally over and the North celebrated its victory. Six months later, in October, 1865, Charlotte went to work in Boston, accepting a position as the secretary of the Teachers Committee of the New England branch of the Freedmen's Union Commission. In this capacity, her job was to recruit, coordinate, and advise teachers working with freed people. Her employment for the Union Commission spanned several years. In 1871, Charlotte returned to the South to teach at the Robert Gould Shaw Memorial School in Charleston, South Carolina. It must have given Charlotte much joy to teach in a school named in honor of her dear friend from Port Royal. The next year, she relocated to Washington, DC, to teach at the M Street School, a prestigious preparatory school for African Americans that was later renamed Paul Laurence Dunbar High School. She remained in this post for two years, and then she accepted a position as a clerk with the United States Treasury Department. Competition for this job was stiff. Out of two hundred applicants, Charlotte was one of the fifteen that were hired. By this time, Charlotte had celebrated thirty-five birthdays.

Throughout her entire adult life, Charlotte had rebuffed romance, devoting herself instead to her work as a teacher, activist, and humanitarian. But when she met Francis James Grimke, a Presbyterian minister, educator, author, and civil rights activist, she knew she had found a kindred spirit. She became his joyful bride on December 19, 1878. Their union was unusual in its day, for she was forty-one years old, and he was twenty-eight.

Francis, known as Frank, had been born into slavery on a South Carolina plantation, the son of his aristocratic owner, Henry Grimke, and Nancy Weston, one of Grimke's slaves. Like Charlotte, Frank lost a parent at an early age; Frank was only three when his father passed away. After his father's death, Frank became the slave of his white half-brother, E. Montague Grimke. For most of his youth, Frank was allowed to live as a free black, but with the outbreak of the Civil War in 1860, E. Montague threatened to return Frank to a lifestyle of bondage. Frank ran away from his half-brother's plantation and joined the Confederate army, where he served as a valet. A short time later, thinking the danger had passed, Frank returned home for a family visit, but he was mistaken. E. Montague promptly ordered the runaway Frank be jailed. During his incarceration, Frank became seriously ill, and he was sent home to be nursed back to health by his mother. Once Frank recovered, E. Montague carried out the threat he had been holding over his half-brother's head for so long—he sold Frank to a Confederate army officer. It wasn't until that January day in 1863, as young Charlotte stood among that proud and exultant crowd in a South Carolina oak grove listening to the reading of the Emancipation Proclamation, that Frank's freedom was finally secured.

Within a few months of their marriage, despite her mature years, Charlotte was thrilled to discover she was pregnant, and on January 1, 1880, she gave birth to the couple's only child, a daughter they named Theodora Cornelia. Sadly, the child died less than five months later.

For many years, Charlotte and Frank devoted themselves to humanitarian causes and civil rights activism. They relocated to Jacksonville in Duval County, Florida, where for four years Frank served as the pastor of the Laura Street Presbyterian Church. In Jacksonville, they lived in a cozy little four-room cottage trimmed with English ivy and blossoming orange trees in the front yard. Upon their return to Washington, DC, Frank became a founding member of the National Association for the Advancement of Colored People (NAACP), and he also served for many years on the Board of Trustees for Howard University. During these years, Charlotte taught Sunday school classes, organized missionary work, and continued to write. In addition, she worked tirelessly for the National Association of Colored Women (NACW), formed in 1896, of which she was a founding member. She was also active in the movement for women's suffrage. Throughout her life, the causes Charlotte chose to support were closely connected to the American ideal that all people are created equal, and that the individual should have control over his or her own destiny.

Frank and Charlotte were happily married for thirty-six years. Near the end of her life, Charlotte suffered a debilitating stroke that left her bedridden for more than a year. Frank was devastated when she passed away on July 22, 1914, in their Washington, DC, home. He mourned the loss of his beloved wife until his own death in 1937.

Sioux Indian reservation teacher Elaine Goodale Eastman, shortly before her marriage to Charles Eastman in 1891. Reproduced by permission from the Sophia Smith Collection, Smith College.

2

ELAINE GOODALE EASTMAN
She Was a Sister to the Indians

'Tis education forms the common mind.
Just as the twig is bent, the tree's inclined.
ALEXANDER POPE

A tall, lean Caucasian woman stood solemnly in the bitter South Dakota cold on the wooden steps of a primitive cabin that served as the White River Day School. Her only concession to the Victorian fashion of the day was her high-necked, floor-length dress, but contrary to the period preference for tightly fitted whalebone corsets, mutton sleeves, laces, and ruffles, this garment was simply constructed and loosely fitted. Over this dress, the woman donned a shapeless, dark coat and a long, narrow knitted scarf. To warm her head, a black felt hat; to warm her hands, a soft fur muff. And she was wore traditional beaded Indian moccasins, which she declared were infinitely more comfortable and practical than the high-heeled, laced-up feminine footgear of the time.

Huddled around the woman, a missionary teacher named Elaine Goodale, was a group of twenty or so dark-skinned Native American children, the little boys clad in government-issued winter coats and the little girls wrapped in plaid Indian blankets. Most of the children had thick scarves curled around long, coal-black braids and tightly secured around their necks and heads. Despite these layers of cold-weather garments, the teacher and her students shivered in the unforgiving frost.

Inside the weather-beaten cabin—a bare-bones, L-shaped wooden structure with slanted roof and clay-brick chimney—the temperature was not much warmer. The one-room schoolhouse was furnished with one small, wooden, lift-top writing desk and a matching curve-backed Windsor chair, which were placed squarely in the center of a raised platform constructed from two-by-four planks. These were for the teacher. The students occupied two identical rows of rough-hewn, unvarnished wooden pews. How did Elaine Goodale, a twenty-two-year-old Yankee blue-blood from Massachusetts, find herself in this shabby, isolated schoolhouse on this desolate patch of reservation prairie?

The young teacher was descended from two aristocratic New England families. Her father, Henry Sterling Goodale, could trace his family tree all the way back to 1632, to an ancestor who landed at Salem. Born in South Egremont, Berkshire County, Massachusetts, Henry was the proud owner of a seven-hundred-acre working farm he christened Sky Farm. Henry was a published poet, and from 1876 to 1879, he also served as a delegate to the Massachusetts Board of Agriculture. Elaine's mother, Deborah Hill Read, known as Dora, was the youngest daughter of a notable colonial family. A born intellectual, Dora had a bright and dynamic mind. She took pleasure in reading, studying, and writing poetry. She was attractive, refined, and somewhat pretentious, with fastidious tastes and a passion for the finer things in life. Henry and Dora fell in love and were married on August 14, 1862.

Elaine was the couple's first child, born October 9, 1863, at Sky Farm. She was named after a character from Arthurian legend and the heroine of Tennyson's narrative poem *Idylls of the King* (Sargent 2005, 1). Three years later, Elaine's sister, also named Dora, was born, and four years after, her sister Rose arrived. Elaine was fourteen when her mother gave birth to the last Goodale sibling, a brother named Robert.

Henry's Sky Farm was located in a steep and rugged region of the Berkshires, high on the side of Fray Mountain. The area was sparsely inhabited, and the nearest church, store, doctor, or post office was a difficult five-mile hike away in the little settlement of Mount Washington. The Goodale family inhabited a rustic brown cottage situated in the middle of a square-mile plot of half-wild meadow just above the bend of a crystal-clear mountain stream. "The old farmhouse, solidly built, sat as close to the ground as a bird to her nest," recalled Elaine in her memoirs (Eastman 1978, 2). The century-old, woodbine-covered Dutch farmhouse featured a steeply sloping roofline and was heated by four fireplaces, supplied with wood stored in a nearby shed. Clothes were scrubbed by hand with homemade soft soap, rinsed in water from an outdoor pump, and hung to dry in the open air. Fresh bread was baked at least three times a week; butter was churned by hand and served with homemade preserves. Homemade sausage and head cheese and dried apples from local orchards also graced the family table.

Elaine's mother, who was an experienced teacher, spurned the local village academy and decided to homeschool the Goodale children herself. Elaine, who could read fluently by the time she was three, was exposed to a progressively demanding program of lessons that emphasized standard and classical literature. The young scholar's literary education included classical poetry, as well as works by Dickens, Eliot, Hawthorne, Gibbon, Macaulay, and Shakespeare. Additionally, the children received intermittent instruction in music, botany, sketching, and—one summer—lessons in Greek from a visiting clergyman. Elaine genuinely admired many of her mother's qualities, especially her love of knowledge, but Mrs. Goodale could sometimes be moody and contentious, and Elaine always felt closer to her father, a loving and patient man who tended to spoil his young daughters (Sargent 2005, 5). Henry was also a former educator, having been employed prior to his marriage as a teacher at the village school in Egremont and later as an assistant principal in a private boarding school in Nassau, New York.

The Goodale children, although socially isolated, lived a happy and contented life at Sky Farm. Elaine and her sister Dora learned very early to call upon their inner resources for entertainment, turning the casual events of the day into a clever story at the dinner table, writing and performing original plays, and creating other diversions to amuse their parents on special occasions. The two precocious little girls composed a handwritten journal they called the *Child's Monthly Gem*, a practice they continued for eleven years, although they changed the name of the publication to *Sky Farm Life* in 1876. Henry, being a published poet himself, recognized the value of his daughters' creative efforts, and couldn't resist the urge to send copies of some of their poems to his literary friends. These poems eventually fell into the hands of Mary Mapes Dodge, a well-known author of children's books and the longtime editor of the popular *St. Nicholas Magazine*. Six poems written by Elaine and Dora were published in the December 1877 issue of *St. Nicholas* under the title

"Poems by Two Little American Girls." One of Elaine's poems, "Ashes of Roses," written when she was only eleven, is the work most often anthologized (Sargent 2005, 6). In 1878, the sisters published *Apple-Blossoms: Verses of Two Children*, which was an instant success, selling nearly ten thousand copies, a significant accomplishment in those days. This success was followed by *In Berkshire with the Wild Flowers*, published in 1879, and *All Round the Year: Verses from Sky Farm*, published in 1881.

Elaine was an idealistic and impressionable fifteen-year-old when, one warm midsummer afternoon, a dashing figure on horseback arrived unexpectedly at the door of the family cottage. The visitor was a famous Civil War hero, General Samuel Chapman Armstrong. General Armstrong had commanded a brigade of African American troops during the War Between the States, and after the war, he had served briefly in the Freedmen's Bureau. Elaine's entire family was instantly fascinated and impressed by their distinguished visitor. Born on Maui in the Hawaiian Islands of missionary parents, Armstrong had come to the mainland to study at Williams College in Massachusetts. When he graduated in 1862, the Civil War was already in full swing, and he promptly volunteered to serve in the Union army.

After the war was won, General Armstrong, sincerely interested in helping the newly emancipated slaves succeed in their new status as full-fledged citizens, persuaded the American Missionary Association to establish the Hampton Normal and Agricultural Institute in Hampton, Virginia. The purpose of this new school was to provide training for African Americans who wanted to become teachers, and to provide those students with vocational opportunities so they could earn the money to pay for their own education. General Armstrong, who was then in charge

21

of the school, casually suggested Elaine should someday consider undertaking missionary work at Hampton.

Five years later, Elaine's parents acknowledged irreconcilable differences in their marriage and separated. Her father sold Sky Farm and accepted a salaried position in New York City, while her mother took the younger children and moved back to her childhood home in Connecticut. Elaine was twenty and suddenly faced with the necessity of financially supporting herself. Prompted by her mother, Elaine accepted General Armstrong's suggestion, which had by then become a job offer, to work as a teacher at the Hampton Institute. As compensation, it was agreed that Elaine would be given traveling expenses, room and board, and a small stipend to pay for her clothing and incidentals. And so it was that in 1883, Elaine Goodale journeyed south to Virginia to become a missionary teacher.

By the time of Elaine's arrival at Hampton, Native American students had been part of the student body for about fifteen years. Their inclusion was brought about through a collaboration between General Armstrong and another noteworthy Civil War veteran, Captain Richard Henry Pratt. At the conclusion of the Civil War, the government had placed Captain Pratt in charge of seventy-two American Indian prisoners incarcerated at Fort Marion in St. Augustine, Florida. Among the detainees were warriors from the Arapaho, Cheyenne, Comanche, and Kiowa tribes. Between 1875 and 1878, Captain Pratt inaugurated an educational program for his prisoners that included courses in English language, religion, craftsmanship, art, and guard duty. He soon discovered that most of his prisoners were eager to learn. When the federal government finally released the detainees, Captain Pratt sought a place where they could continue their education. The only institution that would agree to accept the former prisoners was Hampton. In April of 1878, Captain Pratt sent seventeen of the youngest Native American warriors to the Virginia school, where they were housed together, but separated from the African American students, in a dormitory christened *Wigwam*.

The first students entrusted to Elaine were in a class called "adult primary," a group of about a dozen very earnest, hard-working, and ambitious young braves, some of whom were older than she. Before her employment at Hampton, Elaine had never received any formal training in teaching strategies, but she found this was not entirely to her disadvantage. "I had early learned to think for myself and was handicapped by no stereotyped ideas or prescribed methods in the effort to devise a fresh and natural approach to the unique problem that confronted us in those days," recalled Elaine in her memoirs, *Sister to the Sioux*. "Much hung on our sympathy, ingenuity, and quick appreciation of the struggle to relearn, in maturity, such fundamental tools as a new language, new conventions, new social attitudes. It was a struggle of the will and the emotions, no less than of the intellect, in which both teacher and pupils engaged as pioneers" (Eastman 1978, 19). Her principal, General Armstrong, recognized right away that Elaine possessed considerable natural talent as an educator.

In 1885, after a little more than a year of teaching, Elaine persuaded General Armstrong to arrange an escorted expedition to the Great Sioux Reservation in Dakota Territory in order to learn more about the background of her students. In this endeavor, she was accompanied by another volunteer teacher from Hampton, Florence Bascom, who later established a reputation for herself as a distinguished geologist. The two young teachers were escorted on their tour by two male officers of the newly established Indian Rights Association.

The party traveled first by train across the gently rolling plains to the Crow Creek Reservation. There they attended the annual Seven Council Fires gathering. Afterwards they trekked by buggy over the gummy, clay-rich soil of the gumbo hills to reach the frontier outpost of White River, located on the Lower Brule Reservation. In White River, Elaine was greatly dismayed by the sight of the empty and forlorn little government schoolhouse, a "dreary, paintless, broken-windowed shack" which had been erected as part of a treaty pledge that promised the Indians a school for every thirty children (Eastman 1978, 25). The schoolhouse had never been occupied.

In Pierre, South Dakota, Elaine and her companions boarded a steamboat and continued their travels down the Missouri River, considered by most riverboat captains of the day to be a navigational nightmare. It was, therefore, no surprise when they soon became grounded on a sandbank. The travelers spent the night on deck, entertained by frontier tales from their captain until the vessel could be extricated. Upon disembarking at Fort Bennett, the party traversed the sparsely populated badlands by covered wagon, camping on the road—sometimes in tents, sometimes in a deserted schoolhouse or mission station—until they reached the reservation at Standing Rock. Their itinerary took them next to the Rosebud Reservation and then to the reservation at Pine Ridge, which offered Elaine a distant glimpse of the legendary Black Hills. This two-hundred-mile leg of their journey was accomplished in a buggy, with the addition of a baggage wagon and an extra saddle pony. The party concluded their tour of Indian Territory in Rushville, Nebraska, where they boarded a train for the return to their Eastern starting point.

Elaine came back from this expedition thoroughly convinced that reservation day schools, rather than off-reservation boarding schools, were the best way to educate and assimilate Native Americans. She returned to the Hampton Institute determined to relocate to the Dakota Territory at her earliest opportunity, and render whatever assistance she could to the Sioux tribes living there by becoming a reservation day-school teacher. "Few, perhaps, would care to blaze a new trail in the obscure corner of a wild land, among recent 'enemies' speaking an unintelligible dialect," Elaine confided in her memoirs. "Behind such considerations lurked, no doubt, a taste for adventure and a distinct bent toward pioneering, possibly handed down through a long line of early American forbears" (Eastman 1978, 29).

Elaine was surprised to find General Armstrong very supportive of her plan to establish a day school and community center among the "blanket Indians," a term used to describe Native Americans who continued to live a traditional Indian lifestyle. He wrote a letter of recommendation for her and encouraged her to travel to Washington, DC, to present her proposal to the Commissioner of Indian Affairs, John D. C. Atkins. The political climate at the time favored experimental programs with the goal of helping Native Americans to assimilate, and Elaine found it relatively easy to schedule a meeting with Commissioner Atkins, a whiskered politician from Tennessee who had been appointed by President Grover Cleveland. "I suspect that he was more amused than impressed by his naïve and youthful caller," recalled Elaine. "I distinctly recall his quizzical smile and serio-comic insistence that

I at least call my 'model day school,' where I proposed teaching cooking, sewing, and gardening, as well as English and arithmetic, an 'industrial semi-boarding school,'" she recounted, and, to fit the description, he advised her to serve a midday meal and set up a couple of cots for emergency use (Eastman 1978, 31).

One year later, in 1886, Elaine set out once again for the Lower Brule Reservation in South Dakota to open her day school at White River Camp, located on the western banks of the Missouri River. To Elaine's delight, her friend and fellow teacher from Hampton, Laura Tileston, offered to accompany her on this pioneering venture. Laura was several years older than Elaine, more mature and more experienced socially, and unfailingly cheerful, so her presence on the undertaking was most welcome. Elaine and Laura spent the next three years teaching together at White River Day School, living with their chaperone and a missionary couple in a primitive four-room lodge that served as both a day school and a mission to the local population of about two hundred Sioux Indians.

On the first day Elaine and Laura opened their school, nearly fifty children between the ages of six and sixteen arrived at their door. Not one of them could speak a word of English or read in their native tongue. Because it was not a custom of the Sioux to use last names, each child was enrolled with his or her given name, his or her father's name as a surname, and an assigned English name to make it easier for the teachers to identify their students.

Typical school room etiquette was very formal in those days, but Elaine attempted to lighten the atmosphere by interspersing brief periods of singing, marching, and simple calisthenics. Between lessons, the girls designed patterns for beadwork, and the boys drew horses on their slates. Elaine described her students as well-mannered, respectful, and eager to learn. She found the parents cooperative and supportive.

At noon, the teachers served their students a hot lunch of beef stew or rice with canned tomatoes, light bread or warm biscuits, and occasionally a dessert made of wild fruit or dried apples. This midday meal, which was prepared by the older girls, was very much appreciated because, although Indian families received regular government rations of beef, flour, and coffee, many of the struggling parents were not able to provide nutritious and filling meals regularly in the home.

To supplement her teaching, Elaine instituted a number of community activities, including school picnics, magic lantern shows, and community suppers. Before long, the schoolhouse became the social center of the community. "Elaine was a highly dedicated teacher who entered wholeheartedly into the life of the community she served," records her biographer, Theodore Sargent (Sargent 2005, 29). To further improve her relationships with the Native Americans, Elaine learned to speak the Sioux language fluently. This was highly unusual in a government employee, and it proved to be a significant advantage for Elaine on many occasions. Her deep respect and high regard for the Sioux people fostered a closeness and a level of trust enjoyed by very few of the white people who routinely interacted with American Indian reservation dwellers.

After working at White River Camp for three years, her exceptional skill as a teacher earned Elaine a promotion. In 1890, Thomas J. Morgan, the newly appointed Indian Commissioner, created the office of Superintendent of Indian Education for the Two Dakotas, and he selected Elaine to be the first educator to fill the position. In this capacity, her task was to travel throughout the five Dakota reservations, visiting the more than sixty government and missionary schools within her jurisdiction, writing detailed evaluation reports that indicated specific areas of weakness and offering suggestions for improvement. To prepare for the extensive travels required to complete the task, Elaine requested and received her own team of horses, a wagon, a complete set of camping gear, and a Native American couple of her own choosing to accompany her as driver and cook. When all her preparations were complete, Elaine returned to Dakota Territory in the spring of 1890 to begin the adventure she herself would describe as "a year on wheels" (Sargent 2005, 33).

Elaine typically arrived at a school without any advance notice, often appearing at the schoolhouse door where she would introduce herself to the teacher, and, declining an honorary seat at the front of the classroom on the teacher's platform, she would slip into a chair at the back of the classroom near the door where her presence would not disturb the instruction taking place. "It may be taken for granted that mine was no conventional call some twenty minutes long, ending in a formal handshake and an inscrutable smile," described Elaine. "I gave no less than a full day to each little camp school at each visit, and to every boarding school a week or more" (Eastman 1978, 125). When the situation seemed to warrant it, she would offer to demonstrate a lesson for a couple of hours, and she typically found the untrained teachers gratefully receptive to her suggestions.

After she observed the teachers, Elaine inspected the dormitories, examined the infirmaries, and personally tasted the food that was served. She casually spoke with the students about their school experiences and informally interviewed the parents in their native Sioux language. She conversed with the school matron, the cook, the seamstress, and everybody else that was connected to the school. Then she gave what sincere praise and encouragement she could truthfully offer, together with a few constructive suggestions, and recorded her observations in a carefully written report sent soon afterward. In addition, to help her teachers become better educators, Elaine organized teacher in-service days, the first of their kind in the Indian Service, which featured open discussions, demonstrations of best practices, and presentations by the local missionaries and agency physicians.

It was during this "year on wheels" that Elaine met her future husband, Charles Eastman, and together they witnessed one of the most tragic episodes in the history of Native American relations, the Wounded Knee Massacre. In 1875, when the discovery of gold in the Black Hills triggered a gold rush, the United States government pushed to take back the valuable land that had already been promised to the Sioux tribes. When white settlers expressed interest in homesteading the territory, the government pressed the issue more forcibly. This resulted in considerable resistance from Native Americans, who felt they had already lost so much through their negotiations with the government and were loath to give up the little they had left. At about this time, a Paiute medicine man named Wovoka claimed to have received a vision that the white man would disappear from the Dakota Territory, the buffalo herds would be restored, and the Indians would once again return to their former lifestyle. Wokova's followers created a ceremonial Ghost Dance to celebrate their future deliverance (Brown 1970, 431-432).

The more experienced government officials, reservation schoolteachers, and missionaries felt no threat by these Ghost Dance ceremonies and believed that, if left alone, the Indians' interest in the practices would eventually dissipate. They went about their usual business. The white settlers, however, were deeply frightened, especially the newly appointed agent of Pine Ridge, Daniel P. Royer, whom the Natives scornfully nick-named Young-Man-Afraid-of-Indians. Agent Royer sent several urgent messages to Washington insisting on military protection, and before the snowfalls of early December 1890, nearly thirty thousand federal troops were stationed throughout the Dakota Territory. The presence of these soldiers exacerbated the already tense relations between the Sioux and the settlers.

Further agitation resulted when the agent of the reserva-tion at Standing Rock, Major James McLaughlin, demanded the arrest and removal of Chief Sitting Bull from his jurisdiction. On December 15, the chief was confronted by forty-three federally trained tribal police and was slain while resisting arrest, along with six of his supporters and seven of the tribal policemen. Hor-rified by the violence, Sitting Bull's followers fled the area in a desperate panic and stampeded southward. Some took refuge with relatives led by Sitting Bull's half brother, Chief Big Foot, encamped nearby on the banks of the Cheyenne River. The fugi-tives were captured on December 28 by Major Samuel Whitside and the Seventh Cavalry, who marched his detainees to a campsite on the banks of Wounded Knee Creek. There they were joined by troops led by Colonel James W. Forsyth, bringing the total number of federal soldiers to 470. Forsyth's men surrounded the Indian camp, setting up four pieces of light artillery known as Hotchkiss guns on the surrounding hills. These cannons were aimed directly at the Indian campsite.

The following morning, the Sioux men, women, and children, approximately three hundred in number, were ordered to surrender their weapons. Chief Big Foot, suffering from a debilitating bout of pneumonia, instructed his followers to comply. However, a deaf tribesman named Black Coyote, perhaps misunderstanding what was being asked of him, resisted the surrender of his rifle. A scuffle over the weapon escalated, and a shot was fired. Immediately the soldiers began to shell the camp and shoot the unarmed Sioux. One of the first shells blew up the tipi of Chief Big Foot, instantly killing the startled individuals, both Native Americans and government soldiers, who were standing near it. Terrified, the defenseless men, women, and children began to run for their lives, and, in the ensuing chaos, the alarmed and impulsive soldiers chased down everyone they could see and shot at them indiscriminately. A total of 146 American Indians—eighty-four men, forty-four women, and eighteen children—were slain outright. In addition, twenty-five government soldiers were killed. A later investigation confirmed that most of the soldiers were killed by "friendly fire" (Brown 1970, 444).

Meanwhile, Elaine and her fellow missionaries, Reverend Charles Smith Cook and his wife, Jessie, were stationed not far from the scene. They had decorated the church and rectory in readiness for a series of holiday programs they were planning for the Indian congregations camped nearby. They erected a Christmas tree and decorated the windows and rafters with festive evergreen garlands of native cedar. Above the pulpit was strung a gaily lettered banner which proclaimed *Peace on Earth, goodwill to men.* The teachers and missionaries had completed their tasks of sorting boxes of donated clothing and toys, collecting money for the purchase of oranges and candy, and conducting nightly rehearsals of Christmas carols. "We were marking gifts and filling candy bags on the morning of the twenty-ninth of

December, when the distant thunder of big guns, some eighteen miles away, sent cold shivers down our backs," Elaine recalled (Eastman 1978, 160).

The apprehensive missionaries continued their holiday preparations until later that evening, when horse-drawn wagons bearing the wounded arrived on their doorstep. The government soldiers were taken to a hastily erected field hospital capable of accommodating sixty patients and tended by army surgeons. The Native American survivors, so badly traumatized they couldn't bear the sight of the blue-coated army surgeons, sought sanctuary in the church. The missionaries quickly set up a makeshift emergency hospital. They dragged the Christmas tree out of the building, tore out and removed the altar and the pews, and scattered armfuls of hay on the floor over which they spread quilts and blankets from their own beds. Then they sent for the newly hired agency physician, Dr. Charles Alexander Eastman, a Santee Sioux Indian who had just recently graduated from the Boston University School of Medicine. As the Native American doctor tended to the wounded, Elaine moved among them, murmuring comforting words and serving them coffee, beef soup, and sandwiches made from supplies acquired from the pantry of the nearby Oglala Boarding School.

The doctor was a handsome man, athletic and trim in build, of medium height, with a deep copper complexion, keen black eyes, jet black hair, and a high forehead. The teacher was a tall, slender, graceful woman, with a pretty face, dark eyes, and a thick mane of curly chestnut hair. "It seemed that we were from the first mutually attracted," Elaine confided in her memoirs. "Others have found me cold, distant in manner, and unduly grave, but to him, as he once said, it seemed as if I carried on my heart the sorrows of his people" (Eastman 1978, 169). After their first meeting, Charles, whose Indian name was Ohiyesa ("Winner"), visited her often at the church house. It soon became her habit to accompany him whenever he went on his rounds, carrying food and other offerings to ease the discomfort of his patients who were shivering from the bitter winter cold in their light cotton tents, suffering from exposure or pneumonia. They had known each other only a few weeks when, on Christmas Day, Charles proposed to Elaine and she accepted.

Elaine was twenty-seven, and Charles was thirty when they were married on June 18, 1891, at New York City's Church of the Ascension. The ceremony took place in front of an altar lavishly decorated with palms, roses, and lilies of the valley. Before a congregation of six hundred witnesses, Elaine's father, Henry, gave her away, and her sisters Dora and Rose served as her attendants. The bride wore a white-corded silk dress richly trimmed with ostrich feathers and featuring a long train. To accompany her dress, she wore a simple wreath of small white roses and mountain laurel adorned by a full tulle veil, and she carried a bouquet of lilies of the valley. The groom was attired in full morning dress and wore a boutonniere of white sweet peas. Following the nuptials, a small but elegant private reception was held at Henry's residence at the Windemere Hotel, a home he had fancifully nicknamed *Sky Parlor*. To please his eldest daughter, Henry had expended considerable effort to obtain sprays of mountain laurel blossoms imported from Sky Farm to use as decorations for the reception. The newlyweds spent their wedding night as guests at Sky Farm, in the room in which Elaine had been born (Sargent 2005, 50).

After their honeymoon in the Berkshire Hills, the couple returned to the Pine Ridge Reservation to establish their home.

Elaine resigned her position as the Superintendent of Indian Education for the Two Dakotas, Charles resumed his duties as the agency physician, and the couple started a family. Within the next eight years, four daughters and a son were born to Elaine and Charles.

In 1899, both Elaine and Charles became employed at the Carlisle Indian School, a government boarding school founded in 1879 by Elaine's long-time mentor, Richard Henry Pratt, who by then had been promoted to colonel. Carlisle was the first and most prominent of the twenty-five off-reservation boarding schools created to help Native Americans assimilate to the white man's way of life. Elaine edited the school newspaper, the *Red Man*. Charles checked on the welfare of students who had been placed as apprentices on farms in the area, a practice known as "outing," and also visited western reservations to recruit new students for the boarding school.

Pratt's school was located on a tract of government land west of the town of Carlisle in Cumberland County, Pennsylvania. Originally, the facility was a set of army barracks first built during the Revolutionary War by Hessian soldiers who had been captured at Trenton. Burned down during the Civil War, the barracks were rebuilt in 1865 around their old brick foundations, which were still intact. After the war, the site was virtually unused until Pratt persuaded the federal government to let him renovate the old buildings into the first boarding school for Native American youths. The twenty-three-acre property encompassed a schoolhouse, a gymnasium, a kitchen and bakery, workshops, a parade ground, student and teacher dormitories, a chapel, a refectory, an infirmary, a coach house, stables, stockyards, and a garden. Each year, up to a thousand students from 140 Indian tribes attended the school.

Students were enrolled in classes in the English language, composition, mathematics, history, religion, music, and art. They were also given vocational training in practical skills such as farming, animal husbandry, butchering, bricklaying, tin-smithing, wagon making, shoemaking, tailoring, and carpentry skills. The girls were given training in the domestic arts, which included sewing, cooking, canning, cleaning, waiting tables, and laundry work.

Academic studies and vocational training were sometimes supplemented by traditional Native American activities. "With characteristic thoughtfulness for their health, and suspected probable nostalgia for the wilds, he early established a summer camp in the mountains, at a place called Tagg's Run," Elaine recounted in her biography of Colonel Pratt. "There small parties might live for a few weeks at a time in tents and again roam the woods, hunt, fish, and pick berries. They even cleared a space of brush and roots, dug and planted it, raising fresh vegetables for the camp table" (Eastman 1935, 87).

Elaine deeply liked and respected Colonel Pratt, but she always believed that reservation day schools were better than boarding schools as environments for providing an education for American Indian youngsters. Many historians agree that Colonel Pratt harbored the best of intentions, but in modern times, Carlisle and other Indian boarding schools have generated bitter contro-versy. Most agree that removing children from their homes, some-times forcibly, and sending them great distances away from their families had a severely detrimental effect on the young people. An identity crisis was created when the children were forced to give up all aspects of their indigenous cultures, including their languages, their customs and religious beliefs, their art and music, their native clothing, and even their names. They found it traumatic when they were forced to cut their long hair, a symbolic act of shame and sorrow to a Native American. The highly regimented routine and a military atmosphere were harsh on the youngest ones. Exposure to diseases to which they had no natural immunities, coupled with homesickness and, in some locations, unsanitary conditions, led to a disturbingly high death rate. Furthermore, there are documented cases of physical and sexual abuse in some of the boarding schools. In great despair, some of the youngsters ran away from their schools, freezing or starving to death trying to make their way back to their home reservations. Some historians go so far as to consider Indian boarding schools institutions of cultural genocide (Churchill 2004).

In 1900, after just one year at the Carlisle School, Elaine and Charles once again returned to service on an Indian reservation, when Charles was offered a position as a government physician at the Crow Creek Agency in South Dakota. This job lasted two and a half years, until March 1903, when the Eastman family relocated to Amherst, Massachusetts, where Elaine gave birth to another daughter.

With six children to support and very few opportunities to earn a living in white society, Elaine encouraged her husband to earn money by recording the story of his Indian childhood, offering to help him with the project by typing, proofreading, and editing the manuscript. When it was published, this attention-grabbing book, entitled *Indian Boyhood*, was an instant success, and generated a high demand for Charles as a public speaker. In the sixteen years following the publication of *Indian Boyhood*, Charles published nine additional books about Native American culture, all highly acclaimed. Elaine was essential to his success, for she edited all her husband's manuscripts and made all the arrangements for his lecture tours. During these years, she also published numerous articles and pamphlets about intercultural understanding under her own name.

At about this time, the United States was experiencing a sweeping back-to-nature movement. Americans were beginning to understand that natural environments were a valuable resource, and Native Americans were perceived as the nation's best experts on the natural world. National parks were created to preserve the country's wilderness areas, and youth organizations that promoted camping, such as the Boy Scouts of America and Campfire Girls, were founded and quickly became popular. To capitalize on this mindset, Elaine and Charles opened a summer camp for girls that they named "The School in the Woods," which was located on the shores of Granite Lake in Munsonville in Cheshire County, New Hampshire. This camp experience emphasized nature study, swimming, sports, and traditional Indian skills such as tracking, archery, sign language, beadwork, basketry, and ceremonial dance. The culminating activity of each camp was the performance of an original play or pageant prepared by the campers, organized by Elaine's second-oldest daughter, Irene, who had been traveling with her father on his lecture tours and was earning fame as a gifted performer of Native American songs. The older daughters, Dora, Irene, and Virginia, served as camp counselors, and the younger children Ohiyesa (Junior), Eleanor, and Florence pitched in with the camp chores. The Eastman family operated these summer camps, which were later expanded to include young boys, from 1915 to 1925.

In the final years of the summer camps, Elaine managed them alone, for after thirty years of marriage, she and Charles became involved in a bitter argument over allegations that he had fathered a child with one of the camp counselors. The husband and wife separated in 1921, and they never saw each other again. Charles Eastman spent the last years of his life living simply in a traditional Indian tipi, just as he had done in his childhood, on the north shore of Lake Huron near Desbarats in Ontario, Canada. He died on January 8, 1939, of injuries sustained in a fire that burned down his tipi. He was first buried in Detroit, Michigan, but in the 1960s his body was disinterred and reburied in Sioux Falls, South Dakota.

In her senior years, Elaine continued to be a prolific writer. In addition to the four books for young people about Indian lore that she published under her own name, she also wrote her memoirs, *Sister to the Sioux*, the fascinating narrative about her years as an educator on the Indian reservation, and a biography of Richard Henry Pratt, the founder of the Carlisle Indian School. She published two semi-autobiographical novels, a book of poetry, and numerous essays, book reviews, and newspaper articles. She was actively involved in the Daughters of the American Revolution, the Northampton Chapter of the Women's Club of America, and the Northampton Motion Picture Council.

Throughout her life, Elaine worked tirelessly to help Native Americans learn how to navigate successfully in the white world, while simultaneously striving to improve an understanding, acceptance, and appreciation for the rich and varied cultures of this country's first inhabitants. Elaine Goodale Eastman died of natural causes on December 22, 1953, in Hadley, Hampshire County, Massachusetts. She was ninety years old. Her final resting place is Spring Grove Cemetery in Florence, Massachusetts, near the place where her daughter Dora and her family lived.

Following Elaine's death, two of her daughters donated all of her personal papers, photographs, and manuscripts to the Sophia Smith Collection, a Women's History Archive, at Smith College in Northampton, Massachusetts.

New York City educator Julia Richman, seen here at age 19, was a champion for Jewish immigrants. Circa 1874. Courtesy of the New York Public Library.

3

JULIA RICHMAN
She Was a Champion for Jewish Immigrants

Any genuine teaching will result, if successful,
in someone's knowing how to bring about a better
condition than existed earlier.
JOHN DEWEY

Early one clear, crisp morning, a young lady left her tenement apartment and ventured out onto the bustling New York City street. The woman was dressed in a dark-colored, well-designed, floor-length skirt with coordinating shirtwaist, which featured the characteristic high neckline, closely fitted bodice, and long, cuffed sleeves that were the fashion of the Victorian period. Tasteful embroidery and beaded detail signaled to the casual observer that the gown's owner was a woman of means. The woman's thick, dark hair was twisted into a tidy bun at the back of her head, and she wore delicate pearl ear rings in her pierced ears. The ensemble was well-tailored and stylish, yet respectable and conservative, as befitted a late nineteenth-century schoolteacher.

The outfit seemed too refined for the squalor of the urban street, however, which teemed with excessive noise and mounds of rubbish. A multitude of crude, muddy pushcarts crowded the busy thoroughfare, even infringing upon the sidewalk, creating an unsanitary obstacle course for the ladylike pedestrian. The pushcart vendors called out raucously to potential customers in a cacophony of Eastern European languages—German, Czechoslovakian, Russian, and Polish, among others. A throng of laborers jostled the aristocratic lady as she attempted to negotiate her way through the narrow space available. Horse-drawn wagons spewed clouds of dust (and piles of horse manure) in their wake. The young woman raised a gloved hand to her nose to stifle the unwelcome smells and lifted the hemline of her expensive skirt a couple of inches as she carefully picked her way through the garbage to the schoolhouse door.

The young lady was Julia Richman, a remarkable educator who dedicated her career of forty years in New York City public schools toward improving the educational opportunities and the day-to-day living conditions of these people, these hopeful, intelligent, and hardworking Jewish immigrants from the countries of Eastern Europe, to whom she felt culturally and religious connected.

Julia's parents were Moses and Theresa Melis Richman, German-speaking Jewish immigrants from Prague in what is now the Czech Republic. Moses immigrated to America in 1844 when he was twenty-three years old. Theresa arrived five years later, when she was twenty-six. The two were most likely engaged prior to Theresa's departure from Prague, for they were married immediately after her arrival in New York. By profession, Moses was a prosperous painter and glazier.

Julia was born October 12, 1855, in New York City, the third of five children. Her older siblings included her sister Adeline, born in 1850, and her brother Daniel, born in 1853. Her younger siblings were Isabel, born in 1858, and Bertha, born in 1860. The family lived in an upscale tenement apartment at 150 Seventh Avenue between Nineteenth and Twentieth Streets in the predominantly Jewish neighborhood known as Chelsea. This affluent neighborhood, which today is recognized as a historic district, was built in the 1830s and was characterized by tenements and row houses built in the Georgian, Greek Revival, and Italianate styles.

Julia was about five years old when her father decided to uproot the family from their metropolitan home. Although he was doing quite well, Moses sought better business opportunities. The Richmans relocated to the rural town of Huntington in northwestern Suffolk County on the northern shore of Long Island. In those days, Huntington was a day's journey from New York City. The town was populated by white Anglo-Saxon Protestants of English stock, and the Richmans were the only Jewish family to live there. Unsure how long he would stay, Moses rented both a residence and a commercial space where he opened up a liquor store. Moses stayed longer in Huntington, perhaps, than he originally intended, for six years passed before the Richman patriarch decided to move his family back to the familiar environs of New York City. His motivation for this move is unclear; it may have been prompted by the sense of isolation, or it may have been because of a concern over the rising atmosphere of anti-Semitism. In any case, eleven-year-old Julia adjusted easily to the change.

As parents, both Moses and Theresa were harsh disciplinarians. Julia's father was strict and was not known to spare the rod. Her mother was a perfectionist and insisted that even the smallest task be repeated until completed exactly right. Despite their stringent parental control, Julia's parents found her a difficult child to manage, as she was rebellious and hot-tempered. She was also an irrepressible tomboy, often shirking her household chores to run outside to play all day. Furthermore, she was considered a homely child, with a full face, large brown eyes, freckles, and red hair. Where Julia did excel, however, was in academics. She thoroughly enjoyed school and easily mastered her lessons in reading, writing, grammar, spelling, and geography. She was especially adept at arithmetic. Unfortunately, Julia's parents did not consider these accomplishments particularly impressive.

By the time Julia's family returned to New York, the youngster had made some important decisions about her own future. "I am not pretty ... and I am not going to marry, but before I die, all New York will know my name!" she declared (Berrol 1993, 33). She announced her intention to become a teacher, a decision her father vehemently opposed. In the late 1800s, an eighth grade education was considered sufficient for girls. As Julia entered adolescence, Moses insisted that his daughter follow the more conventional path of marriage and motherhood. After a protracted battle royal, however, Julia finally convinced her parents to allow her to pursue a secondary education.

In 1870, fifteen-year-old Julia enrolled in a two-year course at Female Normal College, the first teacher training institution in New York City. The school was established by an Irish immigrant, Thomas Hunter, in 1870 on Manhattan's Upper East Side. Thomas served as the college's president for thirty-seven years, and in 1914 the institution was renamed Hunter College in his honor. Female Normal accepted qualified young women regardless of their race, religion, or financial status, and the school quickly established a reputation for its demanding entrance requirements and its rigorous academic programs.

In its beginning, classes were held in rented quarters in an armory and saddle shop located at Broadway and East Fourth Street. The learning environment could in no way be described as ideal. Classrooms were divided by curtains, not walls; ceilings were low; the science lecture halls were poorly lit; and the noise from passing stagecoaches and wagons in the street outside greatly interfered with instruction (Berrol 1993, 36). To remedy these conditions, and because the enrollment quickly outgrew the facility, in 1873 the college was relocated uptown to a Gothic structure constructed on Lexington Avenue between Sixty-Eighth and Sixty-Ninth Streets. By then, however, Julia had already graduated.

While at Female Normal College, Julia completed courses in algebra, history, government, physics, geology, botany, English literature, rhetoric, drawing, penmanship, Latin, French, and German. She also received training in innovative methods of instructional pedagogy that de-emphasized traditional teaching methods that relied on memorization and recitation. A model primary school connected to the college gave the neophyte educator the opportunity to gain valuable student teaching experience. Julia was seventeen years old when she graduated fourth in her class in 1872, a member of the first graduating class of Female Normal.

Julia landed her first teaching position immediately after graduation, at the Grammar Department of Public School 59. This sizeable school was located at Fifty-Seventh Street between Second and Third Avenues, in a Lower East Side neighborhood known as Klein Deutschland, or Little Germany. Teaching in the Lower East Side was challenging. In those days, students were separated by gender. Class sizes were huge, with some classrooms accommodating as many as fifty students. Non-English proficient children were placed in entry level grades regardless of their age, until they mastered enough English to be moved into upper grades. The classroom environment was very formal. Students were accustomed to strict discipline and were required to sit silently with their backs straight while the teacher was instructing. Generally, though, students were eager to learn and were encouraged by their parents to do well in school, for a strong belief in education as a key to success permeated the Lower East Side community. Nevertheless, immigrant children were sometimes unruly and could be difficult to manage for a beginning teacher (Sternlicht 2004, 18–19).

Julia was inexperienced, only seventeen years old, and looked young for her age. Her student teaching experience had been with much younger children. These are probably the reasons why Julia found it extremely difficult to maintain discipline in her first class, which was composed of twelve-year-old boys. She was too stubborn to quit, though, which would mean admitting to her father that he had been right to discourage her pursuit of a career. Through trial and error, she eventually mastered the ability to take charge of her students. After two years, in 1875, she was transferred to the girls' division of Public School 59, a position where she found greater success. In total, Julia remained at her first school for seven years.

Despite her challenges with discipline issues in the early years of her career, Julia established a reputation for being a gifted teacher. Her students scored very well on the multiple examinations that were used at the time to measure student progress and teacher competence. In addition, Julia poured her boundless energy into a number of extracurricular activities, particularly athletics, which, as a former tomboy, she particularly enjoyed (Berrol 1993, 51).

It was in 1875, about the time that Julia transferred to the girls' division, that her father died unexpectedly. By then, the family had moved uptown to a tenement apartment on First Avenue and Fiftieth Street. The Richmans continued to occupy this residence after her father's death. As the years passed, one by one her siblings married and moved into homes of their own, until only Julia remained at home with her widowed mother. The arrangement offered plenty of advantages, but also some disadvantages. On the one hand, Julia's mother did all the cooking, cleaning, and laundry; on the other hand, the two women did not get along all that well. Julia was fiercely independent and may have wanted to find an apartment of her own, but the convention of the day dictated that a respectable, unmarried woman live with a member of the family, and observance of this tradition was particularly important for a woman who expected to pursue a career working with young children.

In addition to teaching in the public school, Julia also conducted Sabbath School classes at her synagogue, the Reform Temple Ahawath Chesed, where she and her family were members. With other young women of her temple, she founded the Young Ladies Charitable Union, which organized parties, receptions, and other social events to raise money for the poor. She later became president of the organization. Eventually, the Union became incorporated into the Hebrew Free School Association, the most prominent educational agency on the Lower East Side, and Julia was named a trustee. The Hebrew Free School Association established a settlement house where they offered hot meals, second-hand clothing, basic literacy skills, and religious instruction to the city's poorest Jewish children. The Association also established a Jewish kindergarten, offered English-language classes to newly arrived Eastern European immigrants, and provided vocational training. Through her charity work, Julia demonstrated an amazing competence for leadership, delegating essential tasks and ensuring their completion, securing the contributions of many wealthy donors, and maintaining perfect attendance at meetings (Berrol 1993, 43).

In 1882, Julia was appointed the vice principal of Grammar School 13, located at Second Avenue and Forty-Sixth Street. In 1884, at the age of twenty-nine, Julia was promoted to the position of principal of the girls' division of Public School 77, the first person of Jewish descent and the first Normal College graduate to become a grammar school principal in New York City. Julia's new school was located at York Avenue and Eighty-Fifth Street. She worked in this position for the next nineteen years.

As the daughter of immigrants, Julia believed strongly in the melting pot theory, and as an educator, she believed the role of the school was to help newly arrived immigrants assimilate into American culture. She took this responsibility very seriously. "Ours is a nation of immigrants. The citizen voter of today was yesterday an immigrant child. Tomorrow he may be a political leader," Julia expounded in a 1905 address to the National Education Association. "Between the alien of today and the citizen of tomorrow stands the school, and upon the influence exerted by the school depends the kind of citizen the immigrant will become" (*Encyclopedia.com* 2001). To accomplish the goal of assimilation, Julia felt it was imperative that immigrant children learn English as quickly as possible. She developed an English immersion program in her school, and in addition to basic literacy skills, she also incorporated American history and civics into the instructional program.

During her tenure at Public School 77, Julia also created a progressive program that caused interested educators from all over the world to travel to her school to observe. Some aspects of her model program are common practices in classrooms to this day. One of Julia's innovations was a plan to group students homogeneously. She grouped students into levels of high ability, average ability, and below-average ability, and she placed her better or more experienced teachers in charge of the classes of below-average learners, those students she felt had the greatest need. In this way, Julia theorized, brighter students would be stimulated through increased interaction with their peers, while below-average students would lose their fear of failure because they were surrounded by others functioning at the same ability level.

Another of Julia's innovations was flexible promotion, a practice which reflected the principle that students should not be automatically promoted to the next grade level at the end of each year, but rather they should be promoted only when they demonstrated a mastery of the material at their current level, at whatever time of the year that occurred. This program required frequent testing, and it often resulted in promotions mid-year, but Julia felt the extra effort was in the best interest of the students.

Yet another of her innovations was a campaign to encourage greater parental involvement in her school. For the mothers, she organized a lecture series offering information about hygiene. She formed a women's club which met on Thursday afternoons to listen to speakers, discuss books, or listen to cultural music. For the fathers, she established a highly successful and popular athletic program for boys that, under her leadership, evolved into the Public School Athletic League.

In addition to these professional accomplishments, Julia became active in the Council of Jewish Women, whose purpose was to improve the quality of religious instruction for Jewish youth. Her sisters Adeline and Bertha were also active members of the Council. Julia served as the chairperson for the Committee for Religious Schoolwork from 1893–1899. During this time, with friend and fellow activist Rebekah Kohut, Julia cofounded and edited a children's magazine entitled *Helpful Thoughts*, which was used widely in Reform Jewish Sunday school classes. The publication, designed for Jewish youngsters from age six to sixteen, contained stories, book reviews, puzzles, contests, and an advice column. She also published articles about Biblical history, geography, archeology, and spiritual topics. Julia herself composed many of the magazine's stories, which often took the form of morality tales promoting good citizenship.

Besides this work, in 1897, Julia, realizing that it had been twenty-five years since she graduated from Normal College, determined to update her professional skills. She enrolled in graduate courses at New York University's School of Pedagogy. This private, nondenominational university was founded in 1831 by Albert Gallatin, who served as the Secretary of the Treasury under both Presidents Thomas Jefferson and James Madison. Julia completed her graduate coursework in two years.

On September 16, 1903, Julia was appointed district superintendent for the Lower East Side, still a predominantly immigrant neighborhood. The district encompassed fourteen day and evening schools, twenty-three thousand students, and six hundred teachers. Julia tackled this new assignment with vigor.

She personified the mottos of both her alma maters, "Mine is the care of the future" from Female Normal, and "To persevere and excel" from New York University. She was ambitious, indefatigable, perseverant, and detail-oriented. Her immediate supervisor, Superintendent William Maxwell, described her as an excellent executive, inventive, and creative. Her subordinates found her to be assertive, exacting, and tenacious. The students loved her. They described her as warm and motherly—"an elegant lady, who wore rustling taffeta gowns" (Berrol 1993, 62).

As the district superintendent, Julia continued to advocate her English-language immersion strategies, programs in hygiene and culture, and vocational training. Julia viewed vocational education as a means of escaping poverty, and whenever she could, she developed courses in industrial arts for boys and domestic arts for girls. Since the majority of the Eastern European immigrants and their children who settled in the Lower East Side were of the working class, vocational training programs were extremely beneficial. Many vocational training courses included instruction on the skills required to compete for jobs in the garment industry, the greatest employer of Eastern European immigrants in Manhattan during the late 1800s. Bakeries and cigar-making businesses were other industries that employed large numbers of immigrants (Sternlicht 2004, 29). To be sure, these were sweatshop jobs, where industry laborers toiled long hours under terrible conditions for very little pay, but to these proud and industrious people, employment of any kind was preferable to joblessness.

Julia also pioneered innovative programs to provide educational opportunities for her district's handicapped students. She categorized the students into two groups. Those with "major" needs were children who were blind, deaf, mute, crippled, or mentally retarded. Those with "minor" needs were children who had impaired vision, moderate hearing loss, asthma, heart problems, or emotional disturbances. She established fourteen specialized classes offering modified curriculums to respond to the unique needs of these students. These classes were the fore-runners of modern-day special education programs. Addition-ally, Julia launched school vision testing practices and programs intended to help conserve eyesight, and she established classrooms on school rooftops where students with respiratory ailments could complete their lessons while exposed to the healing proper-ties of sunshine and fresh air.

Julia also turned her attention to a population of young people others referred to as "incorrigibles." These were the students who were delinquent and habitually truant. When they did attend school, they disrupted classes, committed crimes on school property, and had a negative influence on younger students. The usual method of dealing with incorrigibles was expulsion or confinement to a reformatory, but Julia sought a more positive solution. She converted an obsolete building on Broome Street in Lower Manhattan into a probationary school. Public School 120 opened in October 1905, offering programs for 135 boys—a group of the most hardened liars, gamblers, and pickpockets that could be found on the Lower East Side. The teaching staff consisted of six women and five men with special training in psychology who had volunteered for the assignment. Julia and her staff believed that, with a warm and friendly approach, patience, personal atten-tion, and affection, they could change the incorrigibles into pro-ductive and constructive members of society. The school offered small class sizes, two teachers to each classroom, and a collabora-tive learning environment. The school also offered an extensive athletic program with emphasis on sportsmanship and obeying the rules of the game. Corporal punishment, although widely used in other schools at the time, was never used in Julia's probationary school. An evaluation of this innovative program revealed a success rate of about 49 percent, and the undertaking was hailed a success (Berrol 1993, 75–76).

Julia believed her crowning achievement, though, was the opening of her district's flagship school, Public School 62. The new facility featured spacious classrooms stocked with the most modern equipment available for vocational training in manual arts and domestic science. The campus also offered a gymnasium and a rooftop playground, amenities Julia and other educational reformers had long promoted. The school also offered a superlative music program. To Julia's delight, PS 62 earned glowing reports, and once again, visitors from around the world traveled to New York to observe this school's model programs.

In 1906, personal matters claimed much of Julia's attention. The health of her mother took a turn for the worse. As a professional woman with a full-time job and numerous responsibilities to her synagogue and charitable organizations, Julia could not provide the level of care her mother's condition required. It was decided that Theresa would go to live with Julia's younger sister, Isabel, who by then was a widow and an empty-nester. This move left Julia with the need to find a new living arrangement. Fortuitously, at just about that time, rooms became available at a settlement house maintained by the Educational Alliance, the most important Jewish charitable organization located in the Lower East Side. Julia and five of her colleagues seized upon the opportunity to move into the Alliance's vacated living quarters.

Julia's new home was located at 8 Montgomery Street in the

heart of the Lower East Side. The house was a spacious orange brick building constructed in the Greco-Roman style. With financial backing from the Alliance, she converted the building into Teachers House, a residence and study center for professional educators, and a place where principals and teachers in her district could meet with three hired social workers to formulate a plan for improvement in their schools (Commire 2001, 285). Lunches, dinners, and receptions for school personnel were also held there. At the beginning of each school year, Julia used the location to meet with all the first-year teachers under her jurisdiction. Most importantly, Teachers House was a place where educators could meet to discuss and experiment with new and innovative instructional strategies.

Julia worked tirelessly for the Educational Alliance. She was an active member of the board, and was also a member of the most important committees such as the Committees for Education, Social Work, Moral Culture, Religion, and Clubs. Julia's work on the Education Committee emphasized the needs of immigrant adults. The organization offered English-language day classes for immigrant mothers and young children, and scheduled courses on the weekends and at night for those who held down full-time jobs. For working parents, a day care center was established. Julia organized naturalization classes to provide instructional assistance to those who were about to become citizens. A Legal Aid Bureau was set up to provide assistance with legal matters. Career coaching to help adults pass the civil service exams helped the more established immigrants gain positions in government offices such as the post office, the customs house, the police force, and the fire department. Vocational courses such as typing, printing, carpentry, plumbing, and electrical work helped adults secure jobs in finance and building trades. The Alliance also provided informational seminars on physical education and domestic science, and they maintained a gymnasium and a well-stocked library and reading room. Low-cost lessons in violin, piano, and mandolin were made available (Von Drehle 2003, 103). For all these programs, Julia guided curriculum content, hired the teachers, and prepared the educational budget.

The indefatigable educator was always looking for ways to improve the community. In 1908, Julia sought solutions to the problem of Seward Park, a plot of land in the center of the Lower East Side that had been opened as a community playground in June, 1899. Over time, the park had become derelict and fallen into disrepair, taken over by pickpockets, Peeping Toms, and child molesters. Julia presented a practical plan to redesign the park into a safe and useful facility, dividing the area into two sections, one portion for use by mothers and young children, and another section for use by older girls (Berrol 1995, 75).

This same year, Julia tackled another Lower East Side issue, but this time her effort did not yield the desired result. Throughout the streets of Manhattan, thousands of peddlers sold their wares from pushcarts, and the majority of them were unlicensed. Anything from fruits and vegetables to household items and dry goods could be found for sale at bargain prices. The practice was generally tolerated by the area's low-income residents. To many, with low overhead and an easily accessible clientele, these rolling vendor stalls were an important means of sustaining or supplementing the family income. A considerable number of the Lower East Side's cash-strapped residents appreciated the convenience the pushcart vendors offered them in their daily shopping. Julia, however, despised them. She felt they generated excessive noise and garbage, displaced children from potential play areas, and involved law-breaking, particularly licensing and Sunday closure ordinances. Her attempts to enlist support from the local police department and the board of education in clearing away the push-carts were an abject failure. Worse, her efforts provoked an angry backlash from Lower East Side residents; some even demanded her dismissal from her position as district superintendent. The uproar eventually subsided, and Julia was not ousted from her job, but she emerged from the battle feeling emotionally bruised and battered (Berrol 1993, 82–83).

Other ventures yielded more positive results. Julia and her younger sister Isabel often worked together on projects they believed would be valuable to the community. In 1908, they co-authored a book for ten-year-olds entitled *Good Citizenship*. The volume encouraged beliefs and behaviors Julia and Isabel con-sidered essential for model American citizens, emphasizing the importance of respecting and cooperating with policemen and firemen, tips for preventing fires, strategies for curbing conta-gious diseases, and suggestions for keeping city streets clean. Also included were true stories of civilian heroes that were intended to teach children that even an average citizen could accomplish great deeds (Richman and Wallach 1908).

Seeking additional ways to help newly arrived immigrants, Julia undertook two new projects in 1910. In January she per-suaded the Educational Alliance to form a committee that would place agents at Ellis Island to assist and protect young immi-grant women through mandatory immigration processing. In November of the same year, she volunteered to establish another committee to oversee acculturation programs designed for the younger children of recently arrived immigrants. During this time, Julia co-authored six textbooks on mathematics. She also published numerous magazine articles about instructional practices in prestigious publications such as *Forum, Educational Review, School Journal,* and *Outlook.*

Unfortunately, the year 1911 signaled the beginning of some difficult times for Julia. In March 2011, the entire Lower East Side community was shocked and horrified by the Triangle Shirtwaist Factory Fire, one of the deadliest industrial accidents in the history of New York City. This devastating fire claimed the lives of 146 garment workers, mostly Jewish and Italian immigrant women (Von Drehle 2003, 3). The gruesome tragedy was witnessed by hundreds of pedestrians and numerous fire fighters who stood by helplessly, powerless to save the lives of the trapped victims.

Following the fire, in May, Julia lost her mother, who died of old age and the complications of pneumonia. Julia grieved over this loss, but viewed the situation philosophically. After all, her mother was eighty-eight years old and had lived a long and satisfying life. Three months later, Julia's favorite sister, Isabel, passed away after a long and painful battle with cancer. This loss was harder to bear, for Isabel had been the sibling closest to Julia in age, and of all the Richman siblings, these two sisters shared the most in common. As Isabel became progressively more ill, Julia became her primary caretaker, staying with her until the end.

Julia suffered yet another blow a few months later when her longtime associate at the Educational Alliance, Isador Straus, who had been a close friend for over twenty years, and his wife, Ida, were lost at sea when the *RMS Titanic* struck an iceberg and sank on April 15, 1912. The couple, who were German Jewish immigrants, was returning from a family vacation in Germany. Isador had refused to get into a lifeboat as long as there were still women and children to be saved, and Ida had refused to get into the lifeboat without her husband. In addition to Isador and Ida, the maritime disaster claimed the lives of 1,503 of the 2,206 passengers on board (Watson 1987, 49-52).

After enduring all this misery, Julia felt very strongly that she needed to get away from her sorrows for awhile. Throughout her adult life, Julia often enjoyed vacationing in the Adirondacks, and she frequently traveled abroad. She spent nearly every summer in France, and she often visited friends in England or traveled to Berlin to see her niece, Adele Wallach Kaempfer, the daughter of Isabel. To lift her flagging spirits, in 1912 Julia decided to spend her summer vacation in France, her favorite European destination.

She departed New York on June 6 aboard the steamship *Victoria Louise*. The voyage began pleasantly, but a few days after setting sail, Julia became seriously ill. By the time the ship docked in Cherbourg, France, her condition was critical. She was transported to the American hospital in Neuilly, a suburb of Paris, where doctors diagnosed acute appendicitis. She immediately underwent an emergency appendectomy, and for a brief time seemed to be on the mend. A few days following the surgery, however, peritonitis set in, and on June 24, 1912, Julia passed away. She was fifty-six years old. After a brief service at a synagogue on the Rue Copernic, her remains were returned to the United States on the steamship *Lapland*. Her body arrived in New York on July 8, and two days later a funeral service was held at Temple Ahawath Chesed. She was interred near her parents in the Ahawath Chesed Cemetery at Linden Hill in Queens.

On the day of Julia's funeral, the New York City Board of Education ordered the flags of all public schools to be flown at half mast in her honor. To further commemorate the forty-year career of this remarkable educator, Julia Richman High School was opened in 1923 on the Upper East Side of Manhattan, at 317 East Sixty-Seventh Street, between First and Second Avenue. On that momentous day, it appeared that Julia's prediction as an eleven-year-old had come true. She had never married, she had never had any children of her own, but all of New York City knew her name.

Teacher Anne Sullivan Macy, pictured here with Helen Keller, developed innovative teaching strategies for deaf and blind students. 1988.

4

ANNE SULLIVAN MACY
She Pioneered Education for the Handicapped

Life is indeed darkness save when there is urge,
And all urge is blind save when there is knowledge,
And all knowledge is vain save when there is work,
And all work is empty save when there is love.
KHALIL GIBRAN

The teacher slipped inconspicuously into the auditorium through a side door, hoping to blend in with the 3,500 members of the audience. She didn't want the dignitaries assembled onstage to become aware of her presence, especially her internationally renowned student, Helen Keller. The teacher had traveled secretly to Temple University in Philadelphia to attend the ceremony where an honorary degree of Doctor of Humane Letters would be conferred upon Helen. Temple's Board of Trustees had also offered an honorary degree to the teacher, Anne Mansfield Sullivan Macy, but Anne had vigorously declined. "It is a valuation to which I do not consider my education commensurate," she humbly explained, for despite the numerous accolades that Anne had received for her innovative work with Helen, the teacher always felt unworthy of the praise. "All my life I have suffered in connection with my work from a sense of deficiency of equipment," Anne once confessed to Temple President Charles E. Beury (Lash 1980, 596).

When the time came to introduce Dr. Edward Newton, chairman of the Temple Board of Trustees, who was to present Helen with her award, President Beury took the opportunity to inform the audience about Anne's refusal. He read aloud the self-effacing letter she had written to him declining the tribute. In her acceptance speech, Helen paid homage to her beloved teacher, noting that the educator had labored during four long years to assist her deaf and blind student in her pursuit of a bachelor's degree from Radcliffe, but had received no word of recognition for herself on Helen's graduation day.

Seated among the dignitaries on the stage was Governor Gifford Pinchot of Pennsylvania, who was also to receive an honorary degree that day. Moved by the admiration expressed for the extraordinary teacher, Governor Pinchot spontaneously proposed the audience express their opinion on the matter. Instantly the entire assembly leapt to their feet with thunderous applause, insisting that Anne's humility should not prevent Temple University from bestowing upon her the well-deserved honor. On that day, February 16, 1931, "I had the pleasant sensation of thinking that I may after all have been a good teacher," Anne later recalled (Nielsen 2009, 251).

Anne Mansfield Sullivan was born in Feeding Hills in Hampden County, Massachusetts, on April 14, 1866. She was the firstborn child of her parents, Thomas and Alice Cloesy Sullivan. Thomas and Alice were illiterate, unskilled, and impoverished immigrants from County Limerick, Ireland. Most likely their departure from

Ireland was prompted by the Great Potato Famine, but their arrival in the United States was not necessarily the best of timing, for they landed on American soil about 1860, during the turbulence of the Civil War. The year following the birth of Anne, who was baptized Johanna but nicknamed Annie, the couple announced the birth of their second daughter, Ellen, who was nicknamed Nellie. Next came James, who was called Jimmie, in 1869, and then Mary in 1873. In those days, infant mortality rates among impoverished immigrants were high. The couple lost their second son, Johnny, who was born and died on dates that are uncertain; Nellie, who died sometime between 1870 and 1872; and Jimmie, who passed away in 1876. Of the five children born to Thomas and Alice, only two survived to adulthood—Annie and Mary.

In physical appearance, Annie took after her mother, who was slender, with brown eyes and dark brown hair. Her father had blue eyes, a ruddy complexion, and red hair. Both parents spoke with a conspicuous Irish brogue, as did Annie, until she recognized the widespread prejudice against the Irish and consciously worked to rid herself of the accent.

Annie's father, Thomas, was employed as a farm laborer, and the Sullivan family lived in a tenant's cottage on the property of his employer, John Taylor. As a child, Annie enjoyed playing with her siblings and cousins among the ladders, lofts, and stalls in the barn. She especially enjoyed horseback riding and lounging beneath an ancient, gnarled sweet apple tree near their house (Nielsen 2009, 5). Despite these childhood pleasures, Annie developed a deep sense of inferiority over the fact that she did not own pretty dresses, live in a fancy house, or go to school like the young daughter of John Taylor. Annie, a bright and ambitious child, determined to change all that some day.

Her health presented an obstacle, however. When Annie was seven years old, she developed trachoma, a highly contagious disease common in impoverished households where modern standards of personal hygiene were not typically observed. Trachoma is the result of a bacterial infection that causes severe inflammation and layers of scar tissue to develop on the inside of the eyelid and the surface of the eye. Today, the disease is easily treatable with antibiotics, but antibiotics were not available when Annie was a child. Instead, the little girl was left to suffer the intense discomfort, impaired vision, and social stigma of her affliction. In the late 1800s, handicapped children were not educated, so as Annie's eyesight deteriorated, so did her chances of ever going to school. Annie responded to her physical pain and emotional frustration by throwing violent temper tantrums, which provoked her intemperate father to beat her brutally. Sometimes Alice hid her daughter from her husband to steer her clear of the beatings.

The next year, Annie's mother, Alice, succumbed to tuberculosis following a long, drawn-out battle with the disease. Annie had watched her gentle mother's protracted suffering, and it affected her profoundly. As an adult, she recalled that her most vivid memory of her mother's death was watching from a dark corner as Catholic priests from the local church prepared the body for interment. They dressed Alice in a plain brown burial gown, with the single word *Jesus* stitched in white letters across the front, smoothed her dark hair away from her face, crossed her hands, and placed a little cross on a green ribbon around her neck (Lash 1980, 5).

After his wife's death, Thomas became an emotional wreck. He drank excessively, he lost his job and then his home, and finally he abandoned his children. Annie, aged ten, and Jimmie, aged four, went to live nearby with their Aunt Anastasia and Uncle John, while other relatives took in their younger sister, three-year-old Mary. Following her mother's death, Annie became almost completely blind, and Jimmie suffered from a tubercular hip, a congenital condition. It was difficult for Anastasia and John to care for the two handicapped children in addition to their own family, and Annie had a reputation for being a disagreeable, disobedient, and stubborn child. Finally, in February 1876, the beleaguered couple decided they could no longer care for their disabled niece and nephew.

Annie and Jimmie were cast away to the infamous Tewksbury Almshouse in Tewksbury, Massachusetts. Typically men and women were housed separately at the asylum, but Annie became so distraught at the thought of being parted from her brother that finally attendants dressed him in a pinafore and concealed him in the women's ward so the two siblings could remain together. Three months later, Annie's beloved little brother died, leaving her all alone. When she discovered he was dead, Annie screamed, clutched his lifeless body, and cried inconsolably until he was buried.

For four miserable years, Annie lived in Tewksbury's crowded, filthy, and unwholesome environment with other impoverished, orphaned children, in the company of approximately 940 inmates with conditions that included criminal backgrounds, insanity, social diseases, and severe disabilities. Annie slept on an iron cot in a dormitory overrun with rats, and the chamber that housed the bodies of the dead became her play room. It is very likely Annie was sexually abused, repeatedly, at Tewksbury. Those years were so traumatic that, for the rest of her life, she rarely spoke about her experiences there, except to describe them as "a crime against childhood" (Nielsen 2009, 13). But throughout those years, the young girl hung on to one idea: that her only escape from poverty, deprivation, and despair was through education.

One fateful day in 1880, Franklin B. Sanborn, chairman of the Massachusetts State Board of Charities, visited Tewksbury to inspect the facility in response to complaints about the deplorable conditions there. Aware of the importance of this distinguished visitor, Annie trailed Sanborn from ward to ward as he toured the facility, until it became apparent that he was nearing the end of his inspection. Then the nearly blind child flung herself at the blurry body of the inspector and beseeched him to send her to school. At first startled and then profoundly moved, Sanborn ordered that Annie be sent to the Perkins School for the Blind in Boston, Massachusetts. The state would pay for her room and board and educational expenses, a rare opportunity for a charity case.

Perkins, the first school in the country established to serve blind students, was founded in 1829 by educator Samuel Gridley Howe, a close personal friend of Sanborn. The institution was named in honor of another of Howe's friends, Thomas Handasyd Perkins, a wealthy shipping merchant who was visually impaired. Dedicated to educating the blind, Thomas Perkins donated his private mansion to be used as the school's campus and raised funds to financially support the institution. At the Perkins School, Howe earned a reputation as an expert in the field of education for the disabled as a result of his work with Laura Bridgman, a young deaf-blind girl who became his student in 1837. Bridgman is believed to be the first deaf-blind individual to learn language.

Most of the young students who attended Perkins were the daughters of wealthy merchants or prosperous farmers. For the majority of them, their lives were sheltered, refined, and free from want. Annie already struggled with an inferiority complex, which her experiences at Tewksbury exacerbated; among her affluent classmates at Perkins, her status as an orphan and a charity case intensified her low self-esteem. She was nearly fourteen years old and had never attended school. She couldn't read or write at all, and she didn't even know her own birthday. She spoke with a slight Irish brogue, which accentuated the class differences between her and the other girls. She owned no personal possessions, not even a nightgown or a hairbrush. And she was filled with a tremendous mistrust and hatred for almost anyone in authority. Annie was highly intelligent and extremely motivated, but she was also hot-tempered, insubordinate, obstinate, and antisocial, which caused her classmates to reject her and the staff to nickname her "Miss Spitfire."

The environment of the Perkins School offered a stark contrast to Tewksbury. The large, clean classrooms offered expansive windows to let in sunlight, brightly polished furniture, cabinets filled with the most modern equipment, live plants, a piano, and framed pictures on the wall. Over time, Annie lowered some of her defenses and adjusted to life at Perkins, though Miss Spitfire continued to be opinionated, stubborn, and confrontational.

During her six years at the school, Anne underwent several eye operations, offering enough restoration of her sight that she could read printed materials. The long-awaited improvement in her vision did much to lower her level of frustration, and the kindness and understanding of two teachers in particular—Miss Mary C. Moore, the literature teacher, and Miss Cora Newton, the history teacher—went a long way toward reducing her antagonism. Annie's housemother, Sophia Hopkins, who had lost her own sixteen-year-old daughter and was the widow of a sea captain, became like a second mother to Annie, and the school's director, Michael Anagnos, served as a father figure.

The Perkins School offered a modern and progressive education. Annie's instructors avoided the rote memorization and recitation typical of the day and included interactive studies in history, science, music, theology, literature, poetry, and drama. Annie studied the works of Shakespeare, Charles Dickens, Jane Austen, John Greenleaf Whittier, and Sir Walter Scott. She was adept at the literature and history lessons, but could never quite master geometry, a subject she detested. She also rebelled against her physical education classes, which included gymnastics, calisthenics, and military drills, even though her teachers tried to convince her that physical training was imperative to good health. The goal at Perkins was to help students grow up to become independent and self-sufficient adults, so Annie also received what was referred to as "technical" training, which included sewing, knitting, crocheting, needlework, cane-seating, and hammock-making. Emphasis was also placed on learning common domestic tasks, such as mending, basic cooking, and light housekeeping.

Six years after beginning her education at the Perkins School for the Blind, on June 1, 1886, Annie graduated as the school's valedictorian. To her delight, Sophia Hopkins provided the young graduate with formal attire for the occasion. Anne had never owned fashionable clothes, but all her life she yearned for them. Her graduation dress consisted of layers of hand embroidered, scallop-edged petticoats of white muslin, ornamented with a Hamburg ruffle; the dress's elbow-length sleeves had three layers of ruffles and Valenciennes lace. To complete the ensemble, Sophia provided white slippers and a delicate pink sash that had belonged to her daughter. Then she styled Anne's long, dark brown hair into an elegant updo piled high on her head, and she curled ringlets at the temples. Finally, a bouquet of roses matching the color of her pink sash was pinned to her waist. Annie was in seventh heaven. "I gazed at my reflection speechless with delight," she later confessed (Braddy 1933, 93).

At the time of her graduation, Anne was twenty years old. She was acutely aware that she needed to find a way to support herself, but she had very few options. Fortunately, she received a job offer from Tuscumbia in Colbert County, Alabama. The offer came from a former Confederate officer, Captain Arthur H. Keller, and his wife, Kate, who were seeking a young woman to serve as a tutor and governess for their seven-year-old daughter, Helen. The child had been left blind, deaf, and mute at the age of nineteen months as a result of a high fever. The Kellers proposed a salary of twenty-five dollars per month, plus room, board, and laundry services. The offer, considered generous for the time, was a godsend to Anne.

Although Anne had no professional training, no special skills, and no prior experience as a teacher, she accepted the position. She spent six months preparing herself for the undertaking. She learned fingerspelling, she read books on child psychology, and she pored over every report ever published by Samuel Gridley Howe regarding his work with Laura Bridgman. Bridgman still lived on the Perkins School grounds, and Anne visited her frequently to glean whatever strategies she could about how to help a deaf-blind student acquire language. Prior to her departure, Anne also submitted to her eighth eye surgery in ten years, this one to correct a crossed right eye. Michael Anagnos gave her some parting advice: keep her Yankee opinions to herself and keep her temper under control. Finally, the time came for Anne to make the trip to Tuscumbia and to meet young Helen, her new student.

The nervous young teacher felt unsuitably dressed for the journey. Her traveling clothes consisted of a frumpy, floor-length dress of dark blue fabric and an ugly black bonnet made of satin. The only item of fashionable clothing that Anne could afford was a new pair of Victorian high-buttoned shoes that, unfortunately, were too small. Dark glasses protected her red and weepy right eye, which was severely inflamed from her recent operation, not to mention the tears of panic and fear that she had shed along the way. By the time she arrived at her destination, her feet were so swollen that she was forced to wear felt slippers. But she did show off one item of finery: a dazzling garnet ring that Michael Anagnos had given her as a graduation gift (Lawlor 2001, 32).

Anne arrived at Ivy Green, the 640-acre Keller plantation in Tuscumbia, on March 3, 1887. Like most Confederate officers, Captain Keller had lost much of his fortune during the Civil War, but the family still lived in relative comfort. The residence at Ivy Green was a modest white clapboard house dating back to 1820; it was very attractive and pleasingly furnished. English ivy covered the dwelling and the nearby "Little House," where Helen was born, and both structures were surrounded by fragrant honey-suckle, roses, boxwood, mimosa, paulownia, and magnolia trees. The property also featured cotton fields, orchards, horse stables, cow pastures, corn sheds, and plenty of dogs. The Kellers, like Annie, were very fond of dogs.

The first meeting between Anne and Helen was illuminating, to say the least. Right away Anne perceived that Helen possessed a keen and active mind; she was curious, observant, perseverant, and surprisingly quick and accurate as a mimic. But the child was also appallingly undisciplined, lacking even the most basic manners, and at times could become violent. It was evident that the Kellers dearly loved their little daughter, but clearly they had never set any boundaries for the child's behavior. "The greatest problem I shall have to solve is how to discipline and control her without breaking her spirit," Anne commented in a letter to Sophia Hopkins (Lash 1980, 51). When the teacher looked at her young charge, it's likely that she recognized a younger version of herself. Like Annie had been in her youth, Helen was rebellious, combative, and stubborn. Helen's deep-seated frustration over her inability to communicate caused intense rage and terrifying tantrums. The neophyte teacher understood this anger very well, and from her own experience realized that the best way to reach Helen was by demanding obedience and offering love. "Obedience is the gateway through which knowledge, yes, and love, too, enter the mind of the child," Anne theorized (Nielsen 2009, 83).

Almost immediately upon Anne's arrival at Ivy Green, a lengthy and exhaustive battle of wills ensued between the teacher and her student. The initial skirmish came on the day of Anne's arrival, during an unsuccessful attempt to teach Helen the finger-spelled words for "doll" and "cake." The conflict continued the next morning at breakfast. Anne was dumbfounded and repulsed when family members allowed Helen to wander around the table eating from their plates with her dirty hands. Anne vehemently refused to permit this. After evicting the Kellers, including the former Confederate captain, from the dining room, the Yankee upstart rolled up her sleeves and prepared to teach their badly spoiled child a much-needed lesson in table manners. The very physical confrontation included pinching, slapping, and kicking,

but at its conclusion, Helen had learned her first lesson in obedience. She also learned how to use silverware to eat from her own
plate and how to fold her own napkin (Nielsen 2009, 83). Over
a period of weeks and through a series of similarly hard-fought
battles, Anne finally succeeded in transforming Helen into a well-
behaved and compliant child, to the astonishment and gratitude
of Captain and Mrs. Keller.

Next, Anne tackled the task of communicating to Helen the
concept of language, a problematical goal given Helen's limitations. The teacher spent nearly four exhausting weeks of continuous fingerspelling, which Helen imitated without intellectual
understanding. Finally, while pumping water and spelling the
letters "w-a-t-e-r" into her young student's hand, Anne was able to
convey the connection between the fingerspellings and the objects,
and thus the meaning of words, in an emotional breakthrough
moment (Keller 1988, 16). This incident was depicted in a well-
known Broadway play by William Gibson entitled *The Miracle
Worker,* which was later made into a movie by the same name.

Anne's success in teaching Helen was the result of unique
and creative teaching strategies based on her personal observations about how hearing and seeing children learned through
direct and constant interaction. She accomplished this interaction through the only senses available to Helen—smell, taste,
and touch. "Teacher did not tell her little pupil about tangible
objects; she put them into her hand and gave their names—dog,
cat, chicken, pigeon, book, watch, telescope, and so forth, and she
placed my fingers on her face with its infinitely varied expressions. Thus she let everything I could touch display its qualities to
me," described Helen in *Teacher,* the tribute she wrote about her
beloved educator (Keller 1957, 169). But Anne wanted her student

to do more than simply acquire a vocabulary; she wanted Helen to learn how to think. Anne's strategy was to immerse Helen's day with a continuous description of the world around her, in the same way that she would have conversed with her if Helen had been a hearing child. Anne was careful to fingerspell into Helen's hand in complete sentences, a strategy that later was recognized as a being instrumental to Helen's remarkable acquisition of idiomatic language.

In the beginning, there was no formal lesson plan. Helen's curiosity and interest initiated each new lesson. Anne and Helen spent a great deal of time outdoors, engaging in gymnastics, playing in the garden, visiting with various farm animals, wading through streams, smelling wild flowers, and climbing trees. All the while, Anne spelled into Helen's eagerly waiting hand a description of each experience. Years later, Anne reflected that those many hours spent outside helped Helen learn a deep appreciation for nature, and also how to be a keen observer of her surroundings. Anne taught Helen to write with a pencil through the use of a writing board containing grooves shaped like the letters of the alphabet; the device was invented especially for use by the blind. Anne also gave instruction on the Braille alphabet, first using a stylus, to prick each letter into a sheet of heavy paper, and in later years using a Braille typewriter.

From the very beginning, Anne carefully documented every step of her groundbreaking work in letters to Michael Anagnos, who published regular descriptions about the teacher's innovative strategies and Helen's remarkable progress in his annual Perkins report. In this way, Anne and Helen quickly became nationally known figures.

In May 1888, Anne, Helen, and Helen's mother, Kate, traveled to Washington, DC, to the home of celebrated scientist Alexander Graham Bell, the man credited with inventing the telephone. Both the mother and the wife of Bell were deaf, and the innovator spent many years researching ways to help improve the hearing and speech of the hearing-impaired. He was easily able to communicate with Helen using fingerspelling, and he also showed his visitors his newest invention, a special glove with raised letters sewn on each part of the fingers. This "talking glove" enabled individuals to communicate more easily with someone who was blind and deaf. A glove like this would have been particularly helpful to Helen's father, who never fully mastered the skill of fingerspelling (Lawlor 2001, 51). Following their visit with Bell, President Grover Cleveland honored Anne, Helen, and Kate by inviting them to meet with him at the White House.

After their sojourn in Washington, DC, the trio traveled to Boston at the invitation of Michael Anagnos to pay an extended visit to Anne's alma mater. After seeing that her daughter was settled in at Perkins, Kate returned to Tuscumbia. Anne and Helen remained in Boston for a period of about four months so Anne could use the Braille and embossed books available in the Perkins school library to enrich Helen's education. During this time, Anne's instructional program included giving Helen lessons in French. While in Boston, Anne and Helen met many celebrities eager to meet the famous young teacher and her student, including the author Oliver Wendell Holmes, the poet John Greenleaf Whittier, and the author-historian Dr. Edward Everett Hale.

When Helen was fourteen years old, the Kellers decided that Helen should further her education in a specialist school, a secondary school that offers a curriculum focused on a specific subject or skill. Therefore, in 1894, Anne escorted Helen to New York

City, where Helen was enrolled in the Wright-Humason School for the Deaf, which specialized in training deaf students in the skills of lipreading and vocalization. The school, located just west of Central Park at 42 West Seventy-Sixth Street, offered a comfortable, home-like setting that both Anne and Helen found very pleasing. For the next two years, Helen's studies at the Wright-Humason School included arithmetic, English literature, United States history, geography, French, and German.

Although efforts to teach Helen to vocalize were not successful, Helen did learn the lipreading technique she employed the rest of her life. To lipread, Helen would place the index finger of her left hand on the speaker's lips, perpendicular to the lips, and place her thumb on the speaker's throat. Interpreting the vibrations of the speaker's throat and the movement of the lips, she could comprehend at least the majority of what was being spoken. One of the advantages of this technique was that while she was listening, her right hand was free to fingerspell remarks, responses, or questions to Annie (Nielsen 2009, 137).

Helen completed her studies at the Wright-Humason School in October 1896. Anne and sixteen-year-old Helen then traveled to Cambridge, Massachusetts, to the Cambridge School for Young Ladies, where Helen enrolled in college preparatory classes to prepare for her entrance exams to Radcliffe College. This was a daring move, as never before had a deaf-blind person successfully attended college, and Helen's success was dependent upon Anne's competency as an educator. Anne estimated it would take Helen five years to prepare for Radcliffe.

The first year, Helen's courses emphasized languages. When Helen attended her classes, Anne was always by her side, taking copious notes for the young student. Because not many teachers at Cambridge knew fingerspelling and few textbooks were available in Braille, Anne was required to fingerspell most of the lecture notes and books into Helen's waiting hands, and Helen completed her assignments on a manual Braille typewriter. In spite of the obstacles, Anne was triumphant when, after only one year at Cambridge, Helen passed nine of the sixteen hours of preliminary examinations required for entrance into Radcliffe. The exams she passed included elementary and advanced German, French, Latin, Greek and Roman history, and English (Keller 1988, 65).

The second year, Helen's coursework emphasized mathematics, including geometry and astronomy. Because Anne had always detested math, she had not provided Helen with a solid foundation in the subject. As Helen struggled with the material and labored under her accelerated work load, a loss of self-confidence and a high level of stress threatened her health to the point that it was decided she should leave Cambridge. Furthermore, Helen's work load greatly taxed Anne's eyesight, and her physician warned the teacher that if she didn't rest her eyes, she would lose her vision permanently.

To relax and recuperate, Anne and Helen were invited to stay with their close friends Edgar and Ida Chamberlin at Red Farm, their New England estate in Wrentham, Norfolk County, Massachusetts. Anne and Helen enjoyed picnics in the woodlands and meadows and boating in the streams and lakes. Once both women had fully rested, Anne assisted Helen in the continuation of her studies, and a tutor was hired to work with Helen in algebra, geometry, Greek, and Latin.

At last, in September 1900, Helen was ready for college, and Anne accompanied Helen when she enrolled as a freshman at Radcliffe. For the first time, Helen would learn alongside sighted and hearing students. As before, few of the textbooks were available in Braille, and most of the required reading had to be finger-spelled into the young student's hands by Anne. When some of the college professors voiced a concern that Anne might be helping Helen too much, a system was set up whereby all of Helen's tests were administered to her in Braille while Anne out of the room. This ensured that Helen's work was all her own (Lawlor 2001, 88).

The next year, Anne encouraged Helen to write her auto-biography, *The Story of My Life*, and the two women agreed to accept the editorial assistance of John Albert Macy, a tall and personable twenty-five-year-old Harvard English professor who was also the editor of a popular magazine called *Youth's Companion*. John learned the manual alphabet in order to communicate directly with Helen, and together they edited and assembled her college essays into a manuscript for the book. Helen Keller's book was published in 1903 and became an instant success, earning high praise from literary critics and celebrities, including Alexander Graham Bell and Mark Twain. By this time, John Macy had become more than an editor to Annie and Helen; he had become a valued and trusted companion, spending a great deal of his leisure time with the two women.

Shortly before Helen's official graduation from college in 1903, Annie and Helen jointly purchased a home of their own in Wrentham: a small, old-fashioned farmhouse, admittedly a fixer-upper, complete with a run-down barn and seven acres of neglected land. The property cost three thousand dollars and was paid for with philanthropic donations and money earned from publishing Helen's articles and books. The spacious, seventeen-room farmhouse was composed of two stories plus a gabled attic, and it featured plenty of large windows. At the front of the house, a wisteria-covered arbor led to the steps of a long, shaded porch. The sunshine-flooded second-floor bedrooms opened onto a wide, uncovered balcony. John built a primitive fence which surrounded the property, enclosing the apple orchard, hazelnut thickets, and woods of pine and spruce. This allowed Helen to explore a quarter of a mile in any direction unassisted. In this serene retreat, Anne and Helen looked after their dogs, entertained guests, organized their lecture tours, and wrote articles to earn an income sufficient to support their financial needs.

Annie was thirty-six when she and John Macy met, but despite their eleven-year age difference, the young man fell in love with the intellectual, artistic, and witty teacher. They shared a deep appreciation for literature, and John was impressed by her flair for writing, her talent for music, and her aptitude for sculpture. He also admired Annie's commitment to Helen. Although Annie had always wrestled with abandonment issues, wide mood swings, and an inferiority complex, she adored John and trusted him completely. She made it crystal clear, however, that under no circumstances would she ever desert Helen.

Annie and John were married on May 3, 1905, in the living room of the farmhouse at Wrentham. The thirty-nine-year-old bride was attractively attired in a dark blue traveling dress and white silk waist; the twenty-eight-year-old groom was handsomely dressed in his gray frock coat. Helen was the bridesmaid, and long-time friend Dr. Edward Everett Hale performed the ceremony. Annie, who enjoyed a reputation as an excellent cook, made the salads, the punch, and the wedding cake for the reception. In addition, she fashioned a celebratory bouquet of carnations for each of the twenty guests. Following the ceremony, the newlyweds honeymooned in New Orleans (Nielsen 2009, 184-185).

Prior to their union, Annie and John agreed that their home as a married couple would always be shared with Helen, so after the ceremony he moved into the Wrentham farmhouse the two women owned. His relationship with Helen was always agreeable and brotherly. His was relationship with Anne, though, however much love there was between them, was always stormy, largely because of her mercurial temperament, his tendency to drink, and the frequent extended periods of time they spent apart.

In 1908, John purchased a house of his own on the coast in Brunswick, Cumberland County, Maine. Although Annie and John began to spend more and more time apart, the trio spent the summer together there in 1909. When Annie had emergency surgery and came close to death in September 1912, John was faithfully by her side for several weeks, but in May of 1913, John sailed alone on a four-month business trip to Europe, following what Helen described as a "hard" parting (Nielsen 2009, 194). Finally, in January 1914, after nine years of marriage, John and Annie formally separated, and, to Annie's inconsolable grief, John declared their marriage over.

That same year, Annie and Helen hired Polly Thomson, an immigrant from Scotland, to join the household as Helen's secretary and personal assistant. Over the next two years, Annie's health gradually deteriorated to the point where she was bedridden. She was diagnosed with tuberculosis, and at the suggestion of her doctors, traveled with Polly to Saranac Sanitarium, a convalescent facility near Lake Placid in upstate New York, to seek a cure. A short time later, Annie and Polly left Lake Placid and sailed to the picturesque island of San Juan, Puerto Rico. Within a few weeks it was determined that Annie's diagnosis was incorrect; the accurate diagnosis was pleurisy, an inflammation of the lining of the cavity that contains the lungs.

In Puerto Rico, Annie was completely enchanted by the beauty and tranquility of the island, and before long was well on her way to recovery. She and Polly were still in San Juan when President Woodrow Wilson announced America's entry into World War I on April 6, 1917, after Germany declared a policy of unrestricted submarine warfare and began sinking American ships traveling to and from Europe. The two women immediately booked passage on the *Carolina*, the first boat that sailed back to the United States.

Upon their return to the United States, financial hardship forced Annie and Helen to sell their Wrentham property and move to a less expensive home in Forest Hills, Long Island, New York. To pay an ever-mounting stack of bills, Annie, Helen, and Polly traveled to Hollywood in the spring of 1918 to make *Deliverance*, a motion picture depicting Helen's life story. The project, which cost a whopping $250,000 to produce, was a commercial failure, and the women were never paid the salaries they had been promised. In fact, the three had to borrow money to pay for their return trip to New York.

In another financial venture, Annie and Helen turned to vaudeville, making their debut on the circuit in Mount Vernon, New York, in February 1920. Anne had previously rejected offers to work in vaudeville, but Helen was eager to perform. Anne finally acquiesced but insisted the act be dignified. For each performance, the women dressed in embroidered or beaded evening gowns and placed decorative pins or barrettes in their waved hair, a fashion typical of the 1920s. The set depicted a pleasantly furnished room with a fire crackling in the fireplace, French doors leading to a garden, and a grand piano. Anne briefly summarized how she came into Helen's life, the "miracle" at the water pump, Helen's educational accomplishments, and a description of her writings. Next they demonstrated the method of lipreading Helen learned at the Wright-Humason School, Helen gave a short speech, followed by a brief question-and-answer period. The presentation concluded with classical music by Mendelssohn (Braddy 1933, 284).

The appearances were enormously popular, and the audiences were interested and respectful, but Anne was never fond of vaudeville. She objected to what she considered the vulgar company of acrobats, parrots, monkeys, and tap dancers. As her remaining vision continued to deteriorate, her role in the act was gradually reduced, and often the quiet, Scottish-accented Polly substituted for her. By 1922, Polly had completely replaced Anne, who often stayed backstage or remained at home in Forest Hills with her dogs and her books (Lawlor 2001, 137). At the end of a lengthy tour in 1922, Annie and Helen's vaudeville career came to an end when further engagements were not offered, even though the performances had been considered a great success.

That same year, Anne, Helen, and Polly joined the American Foundation for the Blind (AFB) in an effort to raise funds to finance the organization's charitable work for the visually impaired. By 1927, Anne, Helen, and Polly had addressed over 250,000 people in 249 meetings in 123 cities. "The educational value of our work cannot be overestimated," Anne once wrote to philanthropist

Moses Charles Migel, chair of the New York Commission for the Blind. "Indeed, it may be that educating the people about the needs and capabilities of the blind is the most important part of our campaign," she asserted (Nielsen 2009, 228).

By 1927, Anne was sixty-one years old, and the state of her health was becoming more and more precarious. Between the years of 1927 and 1930, she suffered from recurring debilitating respiratory ailments, and her remaining vision deteriorated significantly. Before she lost her sight completely, the ailing teacher decided to write her autobiography, and she hired Nella Braddy Henney, an editor from Doubleday and Page, to assist with the research and organize her papers. Anne and Nella became close friends and remained so to the end of Anne's life.

On August 26, 1932, John Macy, Annie's husband of twenty-seven years, suffered a severe stroke and died at the age of fifty-five. There had been very little direct communication between the still-married couple in over ten years, and they had been separated for over two decades, but John's death was still difficult for Annie to bear (Nielsen 2009, 258). She grieved for him the rest of her life. Four years later, on October 20, 1936, Anne Sullivan Macy died from a coronary thrombosis at her home in Forest Hills, New York. She was seventy. Following a funeral service held in her honor in New York, her ashes were interred in a memorial at the National Cathedral in Washington, DC. She was the first woman to be recognized for her achievements in this way.

Throughout her entire teaching career, Anne had only one student, but her groundbreaking work changed the way the society regards the blind and deaf. "Teacher believed in the blind not as a class apart but as human beings endowed with rights to education, recreation, and employment suited as nearly as possible to their tastes and abilities," recorded Helen in her tribute to Anne (Keller 1957, 79). Anne's creative and innovative strategies established a pedagogical standard for teaching the handicapped that is admired and respected to this day. Most astonishing is the fact that she never received any formal instruction or training as an educator—she was entirely self-taught.

For her achievements, Anne received several awards in addition to her 1931 honorary doctorate from Temple University. She was elected a member of the American Association to Promote the Teaching of Speech to the Deaf in 1892, and in 1915, she was honored with a Teacher's Medal at the Panama-Pacific Exposition in San Francisco, California. Additionally, the Educational Institute of Scotland presented her with an honorary fellowship in 1932, and in 2003, Anne was inducted into the National Women's Hall of Fame.

Educator and historian Carter Godwin Woodson, seen here at age 20, originated Black History Month celebrations. Circa 1895. Courtesy of the New River Gorge National River website, National Park Service, Department of the Interior, US Government.

5

CARTER GODWIN WOODSON
He Originated Black History Month

Teachers are more than any other class the
guardians of civilization.
BERTRUND RUSSELL

The hour was late, but in the Washington, DC, offices of the Association for the Study of Negro Life and History, a distinguished-looking educator and scholar pored over the proofs of his most recent publishing project. The individual was an African American man in his early seventies, possessing a full, smooth face, remarkably devoid of wrinkles; intense brown eyes; a resolute chin; high forehead; receding hairline; and sparse, short-cropped white hair. No smile played upon his lips, for he was a solemn, taciturn man; his eyes projected a penetrating stare, his expression austere. He was dressed in an impeccably tailored pin-striped, three-piece suit, with wide, notched lapels, a stiffly starched white shirt; a tie featuring a bold print was fashioned in a Windsor knot, and his leather shoes were polished to a glossy sheen. He wore no jewelry, not even a wedding ring, for this man was, unquestionably, married to his work.

In stark contrast to the man's well-groomed and dignified appearance, his office was in undeniable disarray. Books, magazines, files, schedules, and personal papers were stacked on every surface—the tops of the bookcases, the wooden filing cabinets, and the little side table, which also held the 1940s manual typewriter. Spread out upon the desk amongst the clutter of incoming mail, photographs, manuscripts, and proofs were several issues of the *Negro History Bulletin,* which he was preparing for distribution to schoolteachers to use in their upcoming celebrations of Negro History Week. This eminent educator and scholar was Dr. Carter Woodson, and the entire operation—the Association for the Study of Negro Life and History, the observance of Negro History Week, and the *Negro History Bulletin*—were just some of the products of his life's obsession, teaching everyone all he could about African American history.

Carter Godwin Woodson was born December 19, 1875, in New Canton, Buckingham County, Virginia. His birth came just ten years after the end of the War Between the States. His parents were James Henry Woodson of Fluvanna County and Anne Eliza Riddle Woodson from Buckingham County. Carter's father and paternal grandparents had been slaves belonging to John W. Toney, the owner of a small farm in Fluvanna County. John Toney's property was located on the banks of the clear blue waters of the James River, about seventy-five miles west of Richmond, the capital of Virginia. Toney's slaves worked primarily as field hands, cultivating crops of corn, wheat, oats, and tobacco. On a small farm just across the river lived Carter's mother. She belonged to a different master.

Although Carter's father was a slave, he was given more autonomy than most. A skilled carpenter, James was allowed to make his own labor contracts with local plantation owners who wanted to hire him to construct such articles as wagons, plows, oxcarts, butter churns, or furniture. James was allowed to set his own fees, but he was required to hand over his earnings to John Toney.

James was a proud man, possessing a sense of independence and rebellion that sometimes caused trouble between himself and his master. Late in the Civil War, James became embroiled in a heated dispute with John Toney, during which the slave threatened his owner's life. Fearing reprisal, James ran away into the woods and escaped to the east where he joined up with a troop of Yankee cavalry soldiers under the command of General Philip H. Sheridan. With his expert knowledge of the area, James became a valuable Union scout, leading the soldiers to storehouses and mills throughout Buckingham County where they could replenish their dwindling supplies. Carter's father told him that he eventually came to serve under the command of General George A. Custer and participated in various battles in the Appomattox campaign that ultimately resulted in the surrender of General Robert E. Lee in April 1865 (Goggin 1993, 5).

When the Civil War ended, slaves everywhere in the South were liberated, and James and Anne Eliza were finally able to establish a home together as man and wife. James was thirty when he married nineteen-year-old Anne Eliza in 1867. Throughout the years of their marriage, their household expanded to include Carter, his paternal grandparents, and all six of Carter's surviving brothers and sisters. These children were Carter's older siblings, William, Cora, and Robert, and his younger siblings, Susie, Edward, and Bessie. Two other children born to James and Anne Eliza died in infancy. Of all the Woodson children, Carter was said to be his mother's favorite.

Although both Carter's father and grandfather were competent craftsmen, lack of work forced them into sharecropping. Nevertheless, in the late 1870s, after saving for many years, James and Anne Eliza were finally able to purchase their own twenty-one acres of New Canton land. Every member of the family toiled long and hard on the farm, but despite all their hard work, they only managed to survive at a subsistence level. Like many West Virginians, black and white, the Woodsons lived in unrelieved poverty. Carter once recalled that his mother would feed her seven children in the morning, not knowing where their dinner would come from. The children often left the table hungry and went into the woods to forage for fruits or vegetables growing in the wild. Carter confessed that usually he went to bed early on Saturday nights because he owned only one outfit, and his mother had to wash and iron it overnight so he would have something clean to wear to Sunday school the next morning (Goggin 1993, 9).

Despite their destitution, Carter's parents instilled in their children a keen sense of morality, a strong character, and the value of religion. As a former slave, Anne Eliza had secretly learned to read and write, and she impressed upon all her children the importance of education. Carter's father was illiterate all his life, but he taught his young son many valuable life lessons. Among these were to be courteous to everyone, but to demand respect as a human being; to never accept a handout; and to never compromise on principles (Goggin 1993, 10).

Carter was largely self-educated; he taught himself to read using the Bible and local newspapers. He briefly attended a one-room schoolhouse where his teachers were his uncles, John Morton Riddle and James Buchanan Riddle, brothers of Anne Eliza. Both uncles were educated at schools established by the

Freedmen's Bureau, a federal agency established by President Abraham Lincoln during the Reconstruction Period. The Freedmen's Bureau provided assistance to freed slaves in the form of housing, food, health care, education, and jobs. The uncles' school was open five months of the year, but Carter was unable to attend regularly because he was needed to work on the family farm. Nevertheless, Carter was determined to complete his education, so he persevered with his studies, in school when he could, or on his own when necessary.

As a teenager, Carter worked outside the home to supplement the family income. At first, he hired himself out as an agricultural day laborer, worked at odd jobs, and for a time drove a garbage truck, but he was continually frustrated by his inability to earn a living wage. In 1892, when Carter was only seventeen, he traveled to Charleston, Kanawha County, West Virginia, to lay railroad ties. A few months later, he moved to Huntington, Fayette County, West Virginia, where his two older brothers had moved, to take a job as a coal miner. He worked in both the Kaymoor and the Nuttallburg mines.

Work as a coal miner has always been backbreaking and dangerous. To unearth the underground coal field, men using picks and shovels removed the surface layer known as the overburden. Then the coal was extracted and shoveled into sacks or baskets to be hauled away manually or in sleds, wheelbarrows, or carts pulled by mules or oxen. Every day, Carter toiled in low-ceilinged mine shafts, laboring for long hours hunched over or crawling through dark, cramped, passages that were hot, damp, and poorly ventilated. Every day he faced the dangers of falling rocks, potential cave-ins, accidental explosions, choking coal dust, and poisonous and methane gases. On at least one occasion he suffered injuries by falling slate (Bennett 2005). Carter spent three grueling years digging and loading coal for a salary that amounted to only pennies on the ton.

While working in Fayette County, Carter spent much of his spare time with Oliver Jones, a Civil War veteran from Richmond, Virginia. Oliver opened a tea room in his home where African American miners congregated in the evenings after work to enjoy ice cream and fruit. Carter listened with great interest to Oliver's customers describe their experiences with slavery, the war, and Reconstruction. These personal narratives inspired him to become a pioneer of oral history later in his life. When Oliver discovered that Carter could read, he persuaded the younger man to read to him each day in exchange for free refreshments.

In 1895, when Carter was twenty years old, he was able to go back to school. He enrolled at Frederick Douglass High School, located at the corner of Sixteenth Street and Eighth Avenue in the historic town of Huntington, Cabell County, West Virginia. Named after the famous African American abolitionist, Douglas High was first opened in 1893 and was the only high school in the region accessible to black students. By this time, Carter's uncles, James Buchanan Riddle and John Morton Riddle, who had been his elementary school teachers, had become instructors at the high school, and Carter's cousin, Carter Harrison Barnett, a graduate of Denison University in Ohio, served as the principal. At Douglass, Carter completed four years of study in two years, graduating in 1897.

Following his high school graduation, Carter enrolled in Berea College in nearby Kentucky. Berea, a liberal arts college, was founded in 1855 by abolitionist John Griegg Fee for the purpose of educating slaves. Financially supported by the American

Missionary Association, the institution offered scholarships to underprivileged students and a work-study program to help defray costs. The campus was situated on ten sprawling acres of land donated by antislavery activist Cassius Marcellus Clay. The college's first classroom was a one-room schoolhouse that also served as a church on Sundays. Berea was the first college in the South to be integrated and coeducational.

It was during his years at Berea that Carter decided to become a teacher in the African American community. To this end, he enrolled in courses in general history, science, sociology, literature, rhetoric, economics, and international law. He also completed advanced courses in Roman and British history. Unfortunately, despite the school's financial assistance, Carter couldn't raise enough money to pay his tuition for the entire year, and he was compelled to drop out at the end of his first semester.

Forced back into the workforce, Carter returned to Fayette County, West Virginia, to the small town of Winona. There he accepted a teaching position in a school established for the children of black miners. Winona is located on the banks of Keeneys Creek, in the highlands north of the New River Gorge. Most of Carter's students lived in primitive shacks with no indoor plumbing. They carried water from the nearby creek, and they brought in wood and coal every night to burn in cook stoves to prepare their meals or heat their dwellings. Most families supplemented their coal mining earnings by raising chickens and hogs and growing vegetables in small gardens. The law said no child under twelve could work in the mines, but some of Carter's students undoubtedly were sent to work anyway, in order to contribute to the household's meager income. Carter empathized with these youngsters, black and white, since his own childhood experiences were very similar. Sons often followed their fathers into the mines, where they continued to work all their lives, but Carter was a living example to his young students that, with education, they could have other choices. He taught in the Winona school from 1897 to 1900.

In 1900, Carter returned to Frederick Douglass High School, where he replaced his cousin, Carter Harrison Barnett, as the principal. The following year, in May of 1901, Carter earned his state teaching certificate, easily passing the required exams in United States history, general history, government, science, Latin, mathematics, algebra, music, drawing, and instructional methods. The achievement earned him a substantial raise; his salary more than doubled, from thirty to sixty-four dollars per month (Goggin 1993, 15). The next year, Carter returned to Berea on a part-time basis, and in 1903, he completed the requirements for his bachelor's degree in literature, graduating with high honors.

Soon after Carter earned this degree, he was presented with an opportunity for adventure: a teaching position on the other side of the world, in the Philippine Islands. America had acquired Puerto Rico and the Philippines from Spain in 1898, a prize of the Spanish American War. Originally, the goal of the war was to support Cuba in its effort to win freedom from Spain. The United States accomplished this in short order, gaining control of Puerto Rico and the Philippine Islands in the process. Before he became president, William Howard Taft was placed in charge of a civil commission to administer the Philippines, and the United States War Department recruited American teachers to colonize the new territory, establish schools, and teach English to the Spanish-speaking Filipinos. Carter welcomed the opportunity to travel, as well as the increase in salary.

Carter passed the civil service exam early in 1903, but the War Department didn't authorize his appointment until the fall. In November he boarded a train on the Union Pacific Railroad from Chicago, Illinois, where he had been enrolled in courses at the University of Chicago, and traveled to San Francisco, where he embarked on the SS *Korea* bound for Hong Kong. After a short layover, he boarded another steamship for the fifty-six-hour voyage to the capital city of Manila. He arrived in the Philippines on December 19, 1903, his twenty-eighth birthday (Goggin 1993, 17).

Carter was assigned to a school in San Isidro, a small village near Manila, in the province of Nueva Ecija. The region, composed primarily of wetlands, was known for its abundance of rice fields. A few wealthy white aristocrats owned most of the property and hired small farmers and sharecroppers to work the fields. Unable to speak Spanish when he first arrived, Carter had difficulty communicating with his students. To overcome this obstacle, he enrolled in correspondence courses in Spanish and French through the University of Chicago, and within a year, he was speaking Spanish and French fluently. Carter taught classes in English language, health, and agriculture, most likely in a one-room hut made of bamboo (Goggin 1993, 16). His salary was one hundred dollars per month, considered generous for the time.

In June 1904, Carter was promoted and transferred to the province of Pangasinan. Located on the western coast of the island of Luzon, the area is a major producer of salt. In fact, the province's name means "land of salt." There Carter served as supervisor of schools, and he was also in charge of teacher training.

American teachers in the Philippines expected to find a tropical paradise, but in reality they faced enormously difficult conditions, especially in the more remote districts. Not all teachers were able to adjust to the tropical climate. Of the new recruits, thirty-eight were forced to return home because of illness, while fourteen others died, most from disease. Carter was not immune to the region's tropical diseases and, in 1906, was among those forced to ask for a leave of absence when he became very ill. Carter's sojourn in the Philippines lasted from 1903 to 1907. He valued his teaching experiences there and always intended to return, although he never did.

When Carter left the islands, he spent some time recuperating at home in the United States and then undertook a six-month tour of Europe, the Middle East, and Asia. During his travels, he visited many foreign schools to observe their instructional methods. He attended lectures at the University of Paris, and he conducted extensive research in the National Library in Paris.

Meanwhile, Carter enrolled in additional correspondence courses through the University of Chicago. While completing these courses, he became a member of the African American fraternities Sigma Pi Phi and Omega Psi Phi. He earned his bachelor's degree in history in 1907 and a master of arts degree in European history in 1908, both from the University of Chicago. For the topic of his master's thesis, Carter examined French diplomatic policy toward Germany during the eighteenth century, using research gathered from his European travels the previous year. Carter then enrolled in a doctoral program at Harvard, where he studied from 1909 to 1912. For the topic of his dissertation, he chose *The Disruption of Virginia*. Four years later, he earned the coveted doctoral degree. Carter holds the distinction of being the first and only African American of slave parents to earn a PhD in history.

Following his graduation from Harvard, Carter settled in

Washington, DC, where he accepted a position to teach in public schools. He was originally assigned to teach eighth grade at Thaddeus Stevens School, located less than a mile from the White House at 1050 Twenty-First Street, Northwest. Named after Pennsylvania's abolitionist congressman, the facility served as a groundbreaking school for African Americans at the turn of the nineteenth century, and in later years, it served white students as well. Amy Carter, the youngest child of President Jimmy Carter, was once enrolled at Stevens School. In 2001, the school was placed on the National Register of Historic Places.

Carter also taught at Armstrong Manual Training School, a vocational and technical high school in Washington, DC. Armstrong School was named after General Samuel Chapman Armstrong, a white commander of an African American regiment during the Civil War. The curriculum at Armstrong Manual emphasized training in industrial arts, crafts, and domestic skills. The school, built in 1902 in the Renaissance Revival style, was located at the corner of First Street and P Street, Northwest. Originally, the school's twenty-eight rooms were built to accommodate three hundred students, but at one time, the enrollment grew to seven hundred. In 1966, this building, too, was placed on the National Register of Historic Places. Notable Armstrong alumni include a number of eminent jazz musicians, including Duke Ellington, Billie Eckstein, Charlie Rouse, Jimmy Cobb, Rick Henderson, and John Malachi. Carter was an instructor at Armstrong Manual during the years 1909–1911.

In his off hours, the young teacher could frequently be seen at the integrated Library of Congress, conducting research for his doctoral dissertation. Even though he was employed, he was still a struggling student. "When I arrived in Washington in 1909 and began my research," Carter later recalled, "the people laughed at me and especially at my hayseed clothes. At that time I didn't have enough money to pay for a haircut," (Bennett 2005).

In 1911, Carter transferred to the M Street School, an academic high school for African Americans. Most of M Street's students were offspring of the city's black elite. These students were financially well-off and academically well prepared. Known for its academic rigor, more graduates from this school continued on to college than any other high school in Washington, DC, white or black. M Street graduates became some of the nation's most prestigious lawyers, doctors, architects, and businessmen, including such notable figures as physician and surgeon Dr. Charles Drew, scientist James E. Bowman, educator Nannie Helen Burroughs, and suffragist and civil rights activist Mary Church Terrell. The M Street School, later renamed Paul Laurence Dunbar High School after the famous African American poet, was located at 128 M Street, Northwest. The impressive three-storied brick building was built in 1891, but in 1915, when enrollment exceeded the capacity of the structure, a new facility was built a few blocks away at First Street and O Street, Northwest. The original building was demolished in 1977.

Those who knew Carter during his years as a teacher at the M Street School described him as a man of medium height; slight build; with large, liquid brown eyes; dark curly hair; and a handsome face. Carter was in the habit of standing guard outside his classroom door to monitor the hallway between periods, a strict and stern disciplinarian who commanded good behavior just from his presence. Despite his austere demeanor, Carter's students recognized him as a talented and dedicated teacher (Goggin 1993,

30). He taught courses in French, English, Spanish, and American history at M Street School for six years, until 1917.

In September 1915, during his tenure at the M Street School, Carter attended the Exposition of Negro Progress in Chicago, organized to celebrate the fiftieth anniversary of the Emancipation Proclamation. It was here that Carter was struck with the idea of establishing the Association for the Study of Negro Life and History (ASNLH). For the next thirty-five years, Carter employed the resources of the ASNLH to study the past, the historical contributions, the mythology, and the literature of African Americans.

At the height of World War I, in January of 1916, under the auspices of the ASNLH, Carter published the first issue of the *Journal of Negro History,* an important vehicle for publicizing the accomplishments of African Americans. He published the first issue himself, with money he borrowed against his life insurance policy (Pyne 1994). The *Journal* was produced four times a year and included articles, essays, and book reviews. In his endeavors to research and publicize the history of black Americans, Carter welcomed the support of local schoolteachers. At annual meetings of the ASNLH, Carter offered teachers opportunities to present papers, and he often published their essays in the *Journal* alongside the research of eminent scholars, both black and white. In this way, Carter recognized the academic contributions of elementary and high school educators (Dagbovie 2007, 47). Not one issue of this important magazine missed its deadline, even during the Great Depression and two World Wars.

In 1918, Carter returned to Armstrong Manual Training School as the institution's principal. In this new capacity, he sought to improve the quality of vocational programs so they would equal the school's strong academic programs. Carter improved teaching methods and masterfully connected vocational and academic subjects. Because so many students needed to work, he established an employment office at the school where students could find part-time jobs while they completed their education. Through this office, over one hundred Armstrong students found employment at the Government Printing Office, the United States Postal Service, the Bureau of Engraving, and the Department of the Treasury. Before any student was allowed to drop out of school, Carter sent teachers to make home visits, urging parents to reconsider their decision (Goggin 1993, 46). During the time that Carter served as principal of Armstrong, he also served as the assistant director of adult education for black schools in Washington, DC. Carter resigned from these positions after just one year, however, because he became disappointed with what he considered to be a lack of support for vocational education (Pyne 1994).

After Carter left Armstrong Manual, he became a professor of history at Howard University, a historically black college located in Washington, DC, established in 1867 by the First Congregational Society of Washington. The school was named after General Oliver Otis Howard, a Civil War hero and the commissioner of the Freedmen's Bureau during Reconstruction. Because Carter was the only member of the faculty who possessed a doctorate in history, he was recruited to develop course offerings in black history. He developed a program of study and taught courses in US history, incorporating into his curriculum the role of African Americans in the Revolution, the Civil War, and Reconstruction. He also developed Howard's first graduate program, which offered a master's degree in the history and culture of the African American. During this time, he also served on the university's curriculum committee, the university council, and the Committee for Student Organizations and Activities, and he continued to edit and write articles for the *Journal of Negro History.*

In 1920, Carter resigned his post at Howard to accept a position as dean of Liberal Arts and supervisor of the graduate faculty at West Virginia Collegiate Institute. The Institute, now known as West Virginia University, was located on a parcel of land granted to George Washington prior to the Revolutionary War for his service in the King's Military. Later the land was owned by Virginia Governor William H. Cabbel, who established a slave plantation on the site. The governor's son, Sam Cabbel, inherited the property and married one of his slaves, Mary Barnes. After the death of her husband, Mary Barnes Cabbel sold the parcel to the state with the proviso that a school for African Americans would be constructed there. In 1891, according to her wishes, the West Virginia Colored Institute was founded on the land. A graveyard on the campus still holds the remains of Sam and Mary Cabbel and their children.

From 1891 through 1915, the school provided its students the equivalent of a high school education, in addition to vocational education and teacher training courses. In 1915, the school began to offer college courses and was renamed the West Virginia Collegiate Institute. Under Carter's leadership from 1920–1922, enrollment increased dramatically, and the school offered new classes in psychology, economics, natural sciences, political science, mathematics, history, philosophy, Latin, Greek, and English. While there, Carter created the first formal course in African American History. Carter accomplished much in the two years he spent in this position.

In 1921, believing that it was very important to provide African

American authors opportunities to publish their academic books, Carter inaugurated a publishing company known as the Associated Publishers. Because of this company, many scholarly books and other works by black authors that were rejected by white publishing companies became available in print.

Collecting and recording information about black history was still a major priority for Carter. Several notable African Americans assisted Carter in his work. In 1925, Carter hired Langston Hughes, who later became a prominent poet and writer, to conduct polls and organize some of his research. He also hired Zora Neale Hurston, a graduate student studying anthropology at Columbia University, to collect African American folklore in her native state of Florida. Carter published some of her work in the *Journal of Negro History* in 1927. Both Langston and Zora became celebrated authors closely associated with the Harlem Renaissance, a cultural movement promoting the development of African American literature, music, and art, which spanned the 1920s and 1930s.

At the height of the Harlem Renaissance, in 1926, Carter launched his first Negro History Week. He was careful to select a week in February near the birthdays of both President Abraham Lincoln and Frederick Douglass. The annual Negro History Week celebrations quickly became popular and included such activities as breakfasts, banquets, speeches, poetry readings, lectures on black history, exhibits, displays, special presentations, pageants, and parades with costumed participants portraying notable African Americans. At Carter's suggestion, a substantial number of the scheduled events were offered to the public free of charge (Dagbovie 2007, 50–51).

One of the most unique aspects about these annual Negro History Week observances was that it was the first mass education program targeted specifically to an audience of black youths, as the campaign was run primarily through elementary and secondary schools. As the observances spread, information about black history provided by Carter was incorporated into their celebrations by teachers in countless schools throughout the country. Each year, Carter created an introductory pamphlet, wrote a short history of the ASNLH, put together a list of suggested topics that could be studied, and compiled a recommended reading list. Carter suggested that students study the history of their own school; collect newspaper articles about prominent African Americans in their county, city, or state; and create a play or pageant that represented every phase of African American life (Dagbovie 2007, 52).

To provide further assistance, Carter introduced the *Negro History Bulletin* in October 1937. Included in the issues were biographical sketches of notable African Americans, simple book reviews, artwork by black artists, plays written by schoolteachers, and discussion questions generated by teachers. Because of its low price, many people could afford to buy a subscription. The publication, which began as eight pages but was later expanded to sixteen pages, was published nine times a year, to coincide with the nine month schedule in schools. Up to the 1940s, the price of a subscription was twelve to fifteen cents a copy; in 1950, the cost had risen to twenty-five cents per copy, still an affordable price. In fact, Carter always sold the subscriptions at a loss, because making a profit was less important to him than maintaining a high readership.

In later years, Carter created more comprehensive teaching kits that included pictures of notable African Americans, stories for young children about black leaders in a variety of academic fields, and study guides for the teachers. He provided these materials to state boards of education, elementary and secondary schools, colleges, black newspapers and periodicals, women's clubs, and scholarly journals. Recipients were charged two dollars per kit, although the cost to produce each kit was $2.50. Schoolteachers were instrumental in raising additional funds to pay for these materials (Dagbovie 2007, 50–51).

For two decades, Carter worked tirelessly to promote the inclusion of Negro History Week in American schools, both black and white. In 1960, Carter's week-long celebration was expanded to include the entire month of February and became known as Black History Month. In 1976, President Gerald Ford formally declared February of every year National Black History Month. Most historians agree that originating Black History Month was Carter's most significant accomplishment.

Among his other achievements, Carter was always in great demand as a lecturer. To schedule his speaking engagements more efficiently, he organized a Lecture Bureau in 1927. The same year, he established a Home Study Department which provided correspondence courses to public school teachers. These courses provided instructional strategies for teaching African American history, literature, philosophy, sociology, and art. The courses Carter originated inspired black colleges and universities to offer similar courses through their adult education programs (Goggin 1993, 87). In addition, Carter corresponded with countless individuals interested in black history from all over the world. He answered their questions, evaluated their academic papers, and provided them with information related to black history. Carter once commented that since its beginning, the ASNLH had served as a "free reference bureau" (Dagbovie 2007, 47).

Carter always declared himself apolitical, but during the administration of President Franklin D. Roosevelt, he consented to serve as a consultant to the Federal Emergency Relief Administration, and he was also employed by the Works Progress Administration to collect slave narratives. Additionally, in 1939, Carter participated in the conference called to examine problems of African American youth which was organized by the National Youth Administration, Division of Negro Affairs, a Depression-era federal agency led by fellow black educator Mary McLeod Bethune.

By 1940, Carter's ASNLH set up a home study program, produced textbooks, subsidized young scholars, and sent investigators to work in international archives. Also, the organization published thirty books by African American authors and was involved in directing studies of African American history in clubs and schools. "The accounts of the successful strivings of Negroes for enlightenment under most adverse circumstances reads like beautiful romances of a people in an heroic age," Carter once declared (Gates and West 2000, 77). Throughout the 1930s and 1940s, Carter increased his outreach programs, sponsored lectures, organized teacher training in-service days, and held educational workshops. He was gratified when boards of education began to incorporate African American history into the school curriculum, white teachers and educational administrators sought his advice, and public libraries purchased more books about black history for their collections.

In 1922, the Carnegie Foundation awarded Carter a $25,000

grant to continue his research and edit the *Journal*. The first thing he did was to apply $2,750 of the grant money to purchase a house, which would serve as both the headquarters of the ASNLH and his residence. The house, located in the historic Shaw neighborhood of Washington, DC, at 1538 Ninth Street NW, is a Victorian row house, possessing three stories and a raised basement. The style of architecture was popular in Washington, DC, during the 1890s. The house lies within walking distance of the African American Civil War Memorial, the Lincoln Theater, and Howard University. Carter lived in this home from 1922 until his death. On May 11, 1976, the structure was designated a National Historic Site and is administered by the National Park Service.

In his lifetime, Carter wrote nineteen important books about African American history. He also donated an extensive collection totaling five thousand items about black history from the eighteenth, nineteenth, and twentieth centuries to the Library of Congress. In June 1926, the NAACP presented Carter with their most prestigious honor, the Spingarn Medal, in recognition of his lifelong endeavors to promote knowledge about African American life and history. To celebrate the achievement, *Time Magazine* published a story about him accompanied by his photograph. In Carter Woodson's honor, every year at Christmas time, an ornament bearing the teacher's likeness is hung upon the White House Christmas tree. In 1994, a life-sized statue of Carter was erected in Huntington, West Virginia, where Carter had once been a student, teacher, and principal at Frederick Douglass High School. Today, he is known as the Father of African American History.

Carter was a solemn and introverted individual, had no close friends, and lived an austere and solitary lifestyle. He was described by those who knew him as idiosyncratic, meticulous, driven, and sometimes didactic (Gates and West 2000, 73–74). He never married or had any children of his own. "I don't have time to marry," he once told a colleague. "I'm married to my work." He suffered a heart attack and died in his sleep on April 3, 1950, at his home in Washington, DC. He was seventy-four years old. His remains are interred at Lincoln Memorial Cemetery in Suitland, Maryland.

Teacher Clara Comstock (second from right), with CAS agents Robert L. Neill and Anna Laura Hill, escorting a group of Orphan Train riders seeking foster homes in the West. Circa 1910. Reproduced by permission from the Children's Aid Society, New York.

6

CLARA COMSTOCK
She Found Homes for the Orphans

*Surely there is enough for everyone within
this country. It is a tragedy that these
good things are not more widely shared.
All our children ought to be allowed a
stake in the enormous richness of America.*
JONATHAN KOZOL

The little band of homeless boys gathered on the sidewalk in front
of the Children's Aid Society offices on East Twenty-Second Street
in New York City. They were dressed in brand new clothes typical
of the Edwardian period: double-breasted jackets, starched white
shirts, balloon-style knickers, long knit stockings, and lace-up
leather work shoes. Some wore a little bow tie, others wore a
snuggly fitting necktie, and some bravely clutched a worker's cap
or felt hat. The chaperones, agents for the Children's Aid Society,
stood nearby; one was a teacher, Clara Comstock. Unusually tall
for a woman, Clara was primly dressed in a mid-length motoring
coat over her high-necked blouse and floor length skirt. To complement her Gibson Girl hairstyle, Clara donned a hat with an

upturned brim adorned with artificial flowers. Her long fingers clutched a set of riding gloves. The boys were nervous, for they were about to embark on a life-changing journey, but Clara and her fellow chaperones were undoubtedly confident, for this was a journey they had undertaken many times.

Clara Comstock was born July 5, 1879, in Hartsville, New York, close to the border between Steuben and Allegany Counties. In those days, Hartsville was a sleepy little village with residents who in earlier days had been employed in a thriving lumber industry, but who by that time were primarily engaged in dairy farming. Clara's parents, Charles and Charity Comstock, came from sturdy pioneer stock, and her father earned his living as a farmer and a blacksmith. A brother, Daniel, two years younger than Clara, rounded out the family.

As a young girl, Clara attended school in the neighboring town of Canisteo, a village of only about three thousand inhabitants situated in the foothills of the Allegheny Mountains. Clara studied at the handsome, three-storied brick building that housed the Canisteo Academy. The coed school was chartered on March 16, 1868, and first opened in September of 1871. Clara graduated from the Academy in 1895 at the age of sixteen, and then spent several years working on her teacher's training courses.

Clara possessed an unwavering optimism for the future and a strong belief in the American ideal of helping others in need. These characteristics guided her choices throughout her entire professional career. In 1903, when Clara was about twenty-four years old, she began working as a teacher at the Brace Memorial Farm School in Valhalla, Westchester County, New York. Her students were New York City "street Arabs," homeless boys who were orphaned, abandoned, or removed from their homes because their parents were deemed unfit or unable to adequately care for them. Many of these waifs became involved in street violence or gangs, but some of them were trying to scratch out a meager subsistence by working as newsboys or bootblacks. The plight of these cast-off kids came to the attention of a philanthropist and social reformer by the name of Reverend Charles Loring Brace.

Charles's father was a history teacher, so Charles believed in the power of a good education and the value of gainful employment. Charles's mother had passed away when he was only fourteen years old, so Charles understood the burden of loss and the advantage of a strong family circle. He was deeply moved by the plight of the more than thirty thousand destitute children of New York City, and in 1853 he founded a charity organization he named the Children's Aid Society (CAS).

The primary goal of the CAS was to provide for the poor, abandoned, and neglected children who were living on New York City streets. Charles always supported and emphasized the importance of self-help programs and believed that one of the best ways to help these youngsters, particularly the older ones, was to establish a network of industrial schools. Industrial schools were boarding schools that provided for the children's basic needs for housing, food, and medical care. In addition, the young people were taught fundamental literacy skills and received some vocational training. Instruction in reading, writing, and mathematics was provided for all of the students. As for occupational skills, girls learned the needle trades, such as sewing, dressmaking, and hat making, and domestic skills, such as housecleaning, cooking, and serving. Boys were taught carpentry, shoemaking, and box making (O'Connor 2001, 86).

By the turn of the century, the CAS had established more than

2,500 highly successful industrial schools in New York City, but Charles had a deep and abiding faith in the healing power of nature. He firmly believed that urban "street Arabs" would enjoy a higher level of success if removed from their seedy, inner-city surroundings and exposed to the wholesome virtues of pastoral environs. Thus, Charles became an advocate for the "farm school." Following his death in 1890, his sons Charles, Jr., and Robert attempted to follow through with their father's vision. And so it was that in 1894, four years after the elder Charles passed away, the Brace Memorial Farm School was established in his honor in Valhalla, Westchester County, New York. It seems natural that Clara Comstock, having been born and raised in the region where the new school was established and having come from a farming background herself, should choose to teach at such a school.

The 150-acre school and working farm, located just an hour by train from New York City, provided homeless boys between the ages of ten and sixteen an opportunity to learn useful farm skills. The boys volunteered to attend the school for a probationary period of up to three months. The students were taught not only practical agricultural skills, but also fundamental literacy skills and some rudimentary life skills, such as how to eat with a knife and fork, basic manners, and personal hygiene. If they worked hard and obeyed the rules, arrangements were made for them to be sent west or south to be employed on farms. The few boys that were considered incorrigible were sent back to New York City, but they were allowed to apply for another probationary period at a later time. By all accounts, though, few of the boys needed the second chance, as they greatly appreciated the comfortable beds, the regular meals, and the compassionate guidance of Brace Farm School teachers like Clara Comstock.

Indeed, compared to the hazards and squalor of street life, the Farm School must have seemed like Valhalla, the Viking heaven. The area offered sprawling fields, verdant trees, gentle streams, and plenty of fresh air. The boys were housed in a square-shaped colonial-style farmhouse, featuring a broad porch, neoclassical columns, a sizeable balcony, and wide-spreading eaves. The house boasted all the modern conveniences, including indoor plumbing, pinewood paneling, and electrical lighting. A classroom was incorporated into the floor plan. After their lessons and farm chores were done for the day, the boys could challenge each other to some friendly competition out on the baseball field. The Farm School provided just the sort of wholesome and healing environment the inner-city waifs needed.

Many of the boys who completed the course of study at the Farm School flourished, enjoying a level of success they might otherwise never have known. In the 1905 annual report of the CAS, Robert Brace described the accomplishments of one former student. The sixteen-year-old had been a three-time runaway from a New York City orphanage and had been barely managing to survive on the streets. "According to his own belief," reported Robert, "if left to his own resources he would soon have drifted into the life of a criminal. At the Farm School his better instincts were aroused. He proved ready to work and apt to learn." Within five years of completing the program and relocating to Texas, the young man was thriving. He had purchased his own cotton farm of thirty acres, had established credit in the local businesses, and had earned a good reputation in the community (Fry 1994, 74–76). Reports such as this must have been very encouraging to the Farm School staff.

Clara Comstock worked tirelessly as a teacher at the Brace

Farm School for eight years, and then, in 1911, she transferred to New York City to work as an agent for the CAS. By then, the general public had embraced the philosophy of Charles Brace that, although the Farm School and the industrial schools were achieving positive results, the best possible environment for destitute orphans was a stable home with a loving family, preferably in the wide open spaces of the West. The region represented the American faith in the power of new beginnings and an opportunity to achieve the American dream (Bernstein 2001, 197). At that time, the states in the heartland of America, states we now call Midwestern, such as Indiana, Illinois, Nebraska, Oklahoma, and Kansas, were considered the West.

Clara was one of several teachers, social workers, nurses, and ministers who were hired to care for the children under the protection of the CAS. As an agent, Clara's job was to select adoptable children from New York City orphanages, escort them by train to destinations in the West and place them in suitable home environments. Between 1854 and 1929, an estimated 250,000 children rode the Orphan Trains in search of homes with good farming families, where they could be fostered or adopted. Between 1911 and 1928, Clara personally escorted seventy-four groups of these children.

Clara's duties were many and varied. After selecting the children for the journey, the kids would be scrubbed clean, given a haircut, and provided with two sets of new clothes. Often these clothes were stitched from recycled bed linens by female students in one of the CAS industrial schools. The Orphan Train riders would wear one of their new outfits on the train, and the other when introduced to potential foster parents.

On the day of departure, train tickets were purchased at group discount rates. To keep expenses down, Clara and her fellow agents would pack many of their own provisions, including foodstuffs such as bread, peanut butter, jelly, ham, cheese, celery, cookies, and condensed milk. Fresh fruit and milk were purchased at whistle-stops along the way. The agents would also bring along extra clothes and other necessities such as medicines, toiletries, sewing supplies, silverware, washcloths, and towels (Warren 2001, 26). During the journey, Clara and her fellow agents would tend to the physical and emotional needs of the children, coaching them on how to make a good impression, helping them with their manners, singing songs, and reading stories.

For CAS agents, traveling cross country with groups of children and finding them good homes was an enormous responsibility, but Clara was up to the challenge. By all accounts, she was competent and hardworking, with a take-charge personality. She could be stern when necessary, but she wasn't a scold, and she didn't hold grudges (Call 1999). Arthur Field Smith, one of the young children accompanied by Clara on an Orphan Train in 1922, was placed with a caring family in Iowa. Although he was only four years old at the time, his memories of Clara are vivid. "She was a very loving person, very sweet and motherly," describes Smith. "She was quick to wipe away tears, and quick with comfort and reassurance. I knew right away she was a very special lady" (Warren 2001, 23).

Eventually the group would arrive at its destination in the West, places as different from New York City as any urban orphan could imagine. Most of the children found homes in Illinois, Ohio, Indiana, Iowa, Kansas, Missouri, and Texas, with a smaller number going to homes in Arkansas, North Dakota, and South Dakota. No children were placed in homes west of the Rocky Mountains. When selecting communities for its program, the CAS deliberately looked along established train routes for flourishing towns of about three to four thousand inhabitants, located in the middle of thriving farmlands. Ideally, the towns would offer good schools, and there would be a college nearby (O'Connor 2001, 105).

Prior to the group's arrival in the town, an agent of the CAS would travel ahead to make the necessary arrangements, which included selecting a location for the meeting or reception, arranging for the public announcements, and organizing a committee of local residents who would screen potential foster parents and act as an advisory board. "The committee was selected from men of various professions," Clara explained in a 1957 speech, "a banker who knew the finances; a minister who knew the church life; a doctor, who saw the home under stress; a retired farmer who knew the community life intimately; a lawyer; and a merchant, who knew their business life. Most important of all," she added, "the editor of the local paper. He gave publicity gratuitously..." (Comstock 1957).

The trips were typically planned so that the train would leave New York on a Tuesday afternoon and reach the destination on a Friday. As soon as the travelers arrived, they would be given some time to clean up, change into their best clothes, eat a meal, and, if possible, take a nap before being shepherded to a local church, hotel, or opera house to meet potential foster parents. The children and the applicants would spend some time getting to know each other under the watchful eye of the CAS agents, and, if an agent believed the match was suitable and the children were willing, the necessary paperwork would be completed and the child would go home with the new family.

On Saturday and Sunday, the agents would make themselves available for appointments with local officials to conduct interviews, collect additional information about the families who had accepted the children, and get some much-needed rest. On Monday, Clara and her colleagues would pay a house call to each family where a child had been placed. The agents would hire a livery team of mustangs with a driver, since there were no automobiles in those days, and go around the rugged countryside, often covering as much as forty-five miles in a single day. Traveling by horse and buggy was rough. "The mud in Missouri used to be so gummy that the driver carried a knife to cut it away, because it would roll up on the wheels," described Clara in her 1957 speech. "There were few bridges, and if floods came, we forded the streams or stayed where we were," she recalled (Comstock 1957). On one occasion, Clara and her driver lost their way in the wild hay country of Nebraska, about twenty miles south of Atchison, on a cold November night. "There were no roads; you angled across the prairie," she remembered. "The driver was a one-eyed man and could not see the trail, and I was too much of a tenderfoot to know it" (Comstock 1957).

Following the exhausting schedule of home visitations, Clara and her colleagues wrote meticulously detailed reports which were sent through the mail to the New York office before they left town. Usually, one to two weeks were required to complete all the tasks required to successfully place each child in the group. "I thought it the most incredible thing imaginable to expect people to take children they had never seen and to give them a home," Clara reflected years later. "The work was a great adventure in Faith. We were always helped and grew to expect kindness, deep interest, and assistance everywhere" (Comstock 1957).

Despite the best of intentions, however, the Orphan Trains did not exist without some controversy. During those days, most of the children were placed out, rather than adopted. Although this practice was intended primarily to protect the children, as it gave the CAS the authority to immediately remove a child from a home if they suspected neglect or maltreatment, it sometimes weakened the bond between the child and the foster parents. Another criticism was that many of the children were not actually orphaned but rather abandoned, legally removed from unfit homes, or surrendered by impoverished parents who often had plans of retrieving their children when their economic situation improved. Orphan Train riders were discouraged and at times even prevented from maintaining contact with their biological families back in New York City, and in some cases, the children were sent West without their parents' knowledge or consent. Siblings who traveled the Orphan Trains together were often separated and lost contact with the only family they had left. Furthermore, many of the older boys were adventure-seeking runaways who claimed to be orphans; they were sent West without any attempts to locate parents who might object to their child's departure.

Additionally, in the early years of the program, as an incentive to prospective foster parents, emphasis was placed on what the child could offer in the way of inexpensive labor. It takes many hands to sustain a working farm, and well-trained farm workers were in short supply in western states. Taking in a homeless youngster filled a need for both the child and the foster parents. When placing the children, though, CAS agents such as Clara Comstock clearly communicated the expectation that the children would be treated with kindness, just like a member of the family, and would be provided proper housing, food, and clothing, some spiritual training, and opportunities for education.

It is well documented that, despite best efforts and high hopes, some of the placements did not go well. Sometimes it was obvious that foster parents were only looking for free laborers to work on their farms or servants to cook and clean their houses. Sometimes personalities clashed or for other reasons the placements were simply not good matches, and either the foster parents returned the children or the children asked to be removed. However, in conscientious attempts to find the best possible homes, agents tried to prescreen prospective foster families through advisory boards, such as the one described by Clara in her 1957 speech. Also, the CAS made vigorous efforts to follow up on each youngster through annual visits by an agent and through letters—one from the family and two from the child each year. If deemed necessary, the children were swiftly removed from their foster homes and either placed out elsewhere or returned to New York. In this respect, Clara was known to be particularly diligent. "Miss Comstock made friends with people in the towns she visited," recalls Art Smith, "but she would be firm with them when necessary. If she thought a child was being mistreated, she would remove the child from that home in an instant" (Warren 2001, 30).

Undeniably, the ultimate goal of Clara Comstock and other compassionate agents like her was to find caring parents willing to provide warm and loving homes for needy children who would otherwise have spent their tender years in the impersonal setting of an orphanage, receiving not much more than custodial care. To a large degree, the hardworking agents were successful. According to published reports, the CAS determined that, in 87 percent of the cases they facilitated, both the adoptive families and the children that were fostered out were generally satisfied with their placements.

There were also several noteworthy success stories. Two

Orphan Train riders became governors. One of them was Andrew Horace Burke, who was elected the second governor of North Dakota (1890–1893), and the other was John Green Brady, who was appointed governor of the territory of Alaska (1897–1906). Two others became congressmen, Henry L. Jost represented Missouri from 1923–1925 and James A. D. Richards represented Ohio from 1893–1895. Another became a Supreme Court justice.

Despite the perceived successes of the program, however, by 1918, the tide of public opinion began to turn away from placing out, favoring instead the idea of assisting impoverished children with "home relief." This involved keeping children with their original families and helping those parents to better care for their kids in their own homes. Additionally, social programs that established welfare, widows' pensions, and health insurance, together with child labor laws and compulsory education legislation were some of the results of these changing attitudes.

Clara Comstock escorted her last group of Orphan Train children in 1928. In 1929, the Orphan Train made its final run when the CAS made arrangements to send three young boys to Sulphur Springs, Texas. Later that year, the stock market crash bankrupted the endowment that financed the Brace Memorial Farm School, but the CAS continues to exist and extends a helping hand to needy children in New York to this day.

After her last journey on the Orphan Train, Clara continued to work for the CAS for two more decades, working for their in-state foster care program. In her later years, she moved into a home on Collier Street in the little town of Hornell, New York. She didn't drive, so she hired her nephew, Alton Comstock, to drive her throughout the countryside to check on children she had placed in adopted homes in the area. Typically she would visit each child at least once or twice each year to make sure that all was going well. Alton once estimated that he drove his Aunt Clara approximately a thousand miles every three months. By all accounts, Clara thoroughly enjoyed these house calls. On one occasion, Alton described a visit to a home where the adopted parents, who were in their sixties, seemed ready to collapse from exhaustion. Clara asked the six-year-old what he had done. The little boy responded, "I just wore 'em out" (Call 1999).

Clara formally retired from the CAS on June 30, 1944, at the age of sixty-five, and returned to the New York village where she had spent her girlhood. Still vital and active, she founded the Canisteo Valley Genealogical and Historical Society and donated her time as a regent for the Daughters of the American Revolution. On May 1, 1956, although she was nearly seventy-seven years old, Clara was recalled from retirement and worked another year and a half for the CAS. At the end of this time, on November 20, 1957, a farewell luncheon was organized to honor Clara for her four decades of dedicated service with the CAS.

Clara Comstock never married or had any children of her own, but during her lifetime, she carefully selected families for more than twelve thousand homeless children. Painstakingly keeping track of them until they reached adulthood, she kept a personal diary and filled several trunks with meticulous records of the children she had placed. She passed away on September 11, 1963, and was buried in Hornellsville Rural Cemetery in Hornellsville, Steuben County, New York. Following her passing, Clara's trunks were sent to the CAS in New York. Decades later, these records became invaluable resources for Orphan Train riders who were seeking information about their origins.

Teacher Eulalia Bourne (far left) with little cowpunchers from Baboquivari School aboard their float for the Tucson Rodeo Parade, 1939. Courtesy of University of Arizona.

7

EULALIA COLLINS BOURNE
She Educated Little Cowpunchers

*I believe that children learn best when given the
opportunity to taste, feel, see, hear, manipulate,
discover, sing, and dance their way through learning.*
KATY GOLDMAN

A flat, horse-drawn hayrack wagon loaded with Baboquivari
Elementary School children and their teacher rumbled down
the route established for the Tucson Rodeo Parade. The rickety
wagon, euphemistically termed a "float," depicted a cluster of
Mexican cowboys enjoying their lunch in the shade of a ramada, a
coarsely constructed shelter made of roughly hewn wooden poles
for support, held together with baling wire, and covered with a
roof consisting of Arizona desert brush. A hand-painted sign proclaimed the entry "Little Cowpuncher—Baboquivari School."

The float portrayed the preparation of a typical meal of
burritos, made with fresh tortillas filled with chinitos-style
beans and cheese, topped with tomato and green chili salsa.
The little girls demonstrated the making of the tortillas using
a traditional comal, a flat iron griddle, over an actual fire of hot

coals centered on a mound of sand. Glass bottles of red, green, and orange soda pop added to the festive display. As the wagon lurched down the parade route, the mouthwatering aroma of the burritos wafted over the hungry crowd. In the previous year's parade, the Baboquivari kids wore their own ranch clothing to represent their cattle country origins, but the crowd of onlookers let it be known they preferred the stylish, glimmering fashions of the more affluent private-school students. This year, the teacher arranged for her little cowpunchers to sport glossy dude shirts in an assortment of bright colors. Denim jeans, cowboy hats, and bandanas completed the improvised Western-style outfits (Bourne 1969, 113-114).

Every aspect of the float had been meticulously planned in advance, and then at the last minute, the carefully constructed plans completely fell apart: The borrowed wagon and horses arrived late. They miscalculated the number and length of poles needed to support the ramada. The coals were not hot enough to cook the tortillas sufficiently. And they forgot to bring a bottle opener for the soda pop. Not to be defeated, the teacher and her students, all twenty-three of them, hastily decorated their entry literally at the last minute, on the morning of the parade. The teacher, Eulalia Collins Bourne, wasn't sure they had pulled it off, but the next morning, she was elated to learn that Baboquivari School had won a trophy: an impressive tray of hammered copper. It was just another triumph for this remarkable country schoolteacher.

Eulalia Collins was born in a sod shanty on her father's homestead in the Panhandle of West Texas on December 23, sometime in the 1890s. The exact year of her birth is a mystery. During her lifetime, she was very secretive about many aspects of her personal life, including her age, but very likely she was born in 1892. Her pioneer parents, Albert and Sabrey Collins, produced a family of five daughters: Eulalia, Bessie, Ruby, Sabrey, and Bernice. As a youngster, Eulalia was nicknamed "Sister" because one of her younger siblings was unable to correctly pronounce her name. For the rest of her life, almost everyone except her students called her "Sister."

When Eulalia was still young, her family traveled to a new homestead in the White Mountains of south-central New Mexico, traveling over the tough western wilderness in a horse-drawn wagon. Her parents valued education, but as a youngster Sister received very little formal schooling. She attended elementary school for only three years—the fifth, sixth, and seventh grades—but she was a bright child and a quick learner. She learned to read by studying the labels on flour sacks and cans of coffee, baking soda, and lard.

In 1907, when Sister was a ninth grader, her parents sent her to a college preparatory school at the University of New Mexico in Albuquerque. At her send-off, her mother gave her five dollars to cover her entire expenses for the year; Eulalia promptly lost the money. She spent the entire school year babysitting to earn money to repay the professor that loaned her the money to buy her textbooks. That year, the young student enrolled in courses in English, history, botany, physiology, algebra, plane geometry, and Latin. Eulalia was a diligent student, earning straight As on her report card, but modern inventions were a puzzle to her. The first time she saw an electric light bulb, she was fascinated by the object, but when bedtime came, she didn't know how to turn the thing off. Frustrated, she finally stuffed the bulb, still attached to its long cord, in a dresser drawer and slammed the drawer shut.

123

When Eulalia was sixteen, in a move she later described as foolish, she married William (Bill) Stephen Bourne, a man twenty-three years her senior (Bourne 1974, 19). The couple were wed in New Mexico on April 22, 1910, moved to Arizona, and set up housekeeping in a friend's tent house. Boarded up on the sides, with a double roof to guard against the extreme desert heat, the tent boasted two rooms plus a screened porch. Bill owned a mining property on the banks of the Humbug Creek, and the crusty prospector spent a great deal of time away from his young wife working his claim. It wasn't long before Eulalia went looking for a way to escape her disappointing marriage. Despite her divorce from Bill, all her life Eulalia kept his name; married or not, she was always known as Mrs. Bourne. Nearly ten years later, on August 23, 1922, Bill Bourne was killed in a shootout with his mining partner in a death that was ruled a homicide. Nobody ever discovered what the quarrel between the two prospectors was about, but after the smoke cleared, both men lay dead.

Eulalia knew that if she were going to survive as a single woman, she needed a vocation. Just about the only job available to women in the rugged outposts of the West was teaching. This suited Sister just fine. At the time, qualifications to secure a teaching certificate in Arizona were minimal. Applicants were supposed to be a minimum age of eighteen, but no proof of age was required. Two days of exhaustive comprehensive exams were required in subjects such as reading, writing, arithmetic, grammar, composition, spelling, American history, world geography, and human physiology. The exams were administered in Phoenix, and Eulalia was determined to pass them.

First, she needed a suitable outfit to wear. She had no experience as a seamstress, she didn't even own a pattern, but she did have five yards of lawn cloth, beige with pink flowers. She designed and sewed a dress for herself and trimmed it with lace from a discarded garment. Then, with ten dollars she borrowed, she walked nine miles to Castle Hot Springs, boarded the stagecoach to Congress Junction, and caught the next train bound for Phoenix. On the evening of her arrival, she had no dinner and no breakfast the next morning, either, but on the first day of her exams, during her lunch break, she passed a bakery where she bought six doughnuts for a nickel. She ate two of them with a glass of water for lunch. The next day, she ate two more for breakfast, and the last night she was in Phoenix, she ate the last two for her dinner (Bourne1974, 15–16).

When Eulalia received her exam results, she discovered with delight that she had scored well on the sections related to reading, language, and physiology, but she conceded she could have done better on the math sections. For this reason, she was given a Second Grade Certificate, valid for only two years. Two years later, when taking the exams to renew her license, she scored well enough on the math sections to earn a coveted First Grade Certificate, renewable every four years.

Just before the outbreak of World War I in Europe, Eulalia accepted her first teaching position, in a country school in the picturesque village of Beaver Creek, Verde Valley, in Yavapai County. Accompanied by her fifteen-year-old sister, Ruby, Eulalia traveled to Prescott, where they boarded a train to Dewey, then took the stagecoach to Camp Verde. Upon their arrival, the new teacher discovered—to her dismay—that no housing arrangements had been made for them. The school board expected them to camp at the schoolhouse. On credit, Sister purchased a tent, a little cook stove, a bedspring and mattress, some kitchen utensils, some bedding, and a few groceries at the local general store. She was able to pay the bill a little each month from her salary, which was eighty dollars per month. With their equipment and their provisions, Sister and Ruby were ready to settle into the one-room schoolhouse that would become their home.

A first look at the shabby little Beaver Creek schoolhouse did not generate much enthusiasm. The one-room structure was built of unpainted, weathered boards, and not a tree or blade of grass grew anywhere near it. But Eulalia found the building's interior satisfactory. The room featured a ceiling made of tongue-and-groove lumber that had been varnished, and it boasted two windows on the east-facing wall, plenty of blackboards, a teacher's desk, shelves for books and supplies, and a tall heating stove. An American flag (with forty-eight stars) and a faded portrait of President George Washington decorated the classroom walls.

Including Ruby, Eulalia had ten students that year, the minimum required number. With no prior training in methodology, the novice teacher created a curriculum she hoped would capture the attention of her fidgety students. She started each day with singing. To teach the students language, reading, and punctuation, she showed them how to create homemade songbooks by copying the lyrics of popular and patriotic songs from the blackboard. She led the students in choral recitations of poems which the students learned by heart as "memory gems." She read books and stories aloud to them in dramatic performances that made the kids beg for more. She organized spelling bees and Friday after-noon programs where students recited poems, dialogues, and readings for their parents. During recess, she went outside with the students and played running games with them that required speed, endurance, and alertness. "I out-ran all the girls and three of the boys," Eulalia recalled. "I had splendid energy and spent it every day" (Bourne 1974, 33).

At the conclusion of the school year, Sister and Ruby moved for the summer to the nearby ranch of Harry and Frances Griscom. There they tended the vegetable garden, labored over the house-cleaning and the laundry, and worked in the kitchen to feed as many as twenty-five hired hands that worked in the Griscoms' alfalfa fields. In their off hours, the sisters and some of the hired ranch hands would entertain themselves with picnics, swimming, horseback riding, and community dances. That summer, three college boys from Yale visited the Griscom Ranch for a few weeks. The boys taught Sister and Ruby the one step, a new jazz dance that was all the rage. The young ladies thought the dance was modern and exciting, but most of the locals, including Charles R. Chestnut, the clerk of the school board, judged the "rag" to be vulgar and indecent. He sternly warned Eulalia that if she were ever caught dancing the one step, it would be the end of her job in Beaver Creek. The fun-loving teacher obeyed the edict, at least in public. In private, however, she and Ruby continued to kick up their heels.

When Eulalia and Ruby returned to school in the fall of 1915, they were accompanied by their sister, Sabrey, who was added to the attendance roll. The school had been relocated to an old pioneer dwelling known as the Frederick House, located on Little

Beaver near where it merged with Beaver Creek. The house's sizeable living room with the welcoming fireplace was turned into the classroom and furnished with old-fashioned student desks. Eulalia felt there was not enough blackboard space to accommodate her teaching style and the desks were rather rickety, but otherwise the site was suitable. Frederick House also served as living quarters for the three sisters. Ruby and Sabrey slept in the bedroom, and Eulalia slept in the kitchen on a cot.

That year, including her two sisters, Eulalia served twenty-three students. Because her student body suddenly included four ninth graders, her curriculum load expanded from elementary to high school. This presented quite a challenge to the neophyte teacher. Despite the increased workload, throughout the year, Sister organized her customary Friday afternoon programs with the usual recitations, songs, and dialogues, and two new ventures for the entertainment of the community: the Beaver Creek Literary Society and a series of Saturday night debates. The debates, which attracted an enthusiastic audience, always culminated with dancing.

Everybody at the school had heard rumors about the new jazz dance the boys from Yale had taught Sister and Ruby the previous summer. In March, at a birthday party some of her students attended, the kids begged their spirited teacher to show them the dance. After considerable urging, Eulalia and Ruby demonstrated the one step to the tune of "Too Much Mustard." Word quickly got back to the clerk of the school board, and, the next morning, just before recess, a furious Charles Chestnut drove his heavy farm wagon pulled by his huge draft horses over to the Frederick House. He brought his rig to a screeching halt, stomped into the classroom, and ordered his three children to get out of the school and into the buggy. He fired Eulalia on the spot and angrily drove away. The chastened teacher was allowed to finish the term, but the Chestnut children did not return to school again until Sister was gone (Bourne 1974, 56–57).

Eulalia left Beaver Creek with sorrow and regret. She worried about her ability to provide for herself and her sisters and was relieved when she was offered a teaching position in Helvetia, an isolated copper mining camp located in the foothills of the Santa Rita Mountains in Pima County, south of Tucson, Arizona. Traveling to Helvetia in a buckboard wagon over rough, rocky, neglected roads, her first impressions of the old mining camp were disappointing. She wasn't the least impressed by the semiarid desert flats of prickly cactus, greasewood, and stunted shrubs. She longed for the green grass, verdant fields, and refreshing brook of Beaver Creek. Despite her disenchantment, Sister determined to make a success of this new opportunity and resolved not to repeat her previous mistakes.

The students in Helvetia's crumbling, weathered schoolhouse were predominantly Mexican American. Almost none of them spoke English, and Eulalia did not speak Spanish. This language barrier presented a huge challenge for Sister, who intuitively understood that to teach successfully, she had to earn the trust and win the cooperation of the children. "I resolved to get to know them, to understand them, and to influence them," the teacher reminisced. "To do this, as missionaries have done throughout history, I had to learn their language. I saw that right away. To teach English I had to learn Spanish," she concluded (Bourne 1974, 95).

Her decision presented a problem, however. Arizona law prohibited the use of Spanish at school. Throughout the state, bilingual children were discouraged, even punished, for speaking their native language. Defiantly, Eulalia disregarded the statute, and after acquiring mail-order Spanish grammar books from a bookstore in Los Angeles, she spent every evening in her room poring over the vocabulary words, phrases, and sentences by the light of her kerosene lamp. Then she set aside the last five minutes of each school day to encourage her students to teach her their language. This give-and-take strategy worked. Very quickly the kids were entirely charmed by their new maestra (teacher), and their English-language acquisition grew by leaps and bounds.

It was in Helvetia that twenty-two-year-old Eulalia met her second husband, thirty-two-year-old Ernest O'Daugherty. An immigrant born in Ireland, he had traveled first to Canada, then to San Francisco, and eventually landed in Arizona, where he found employment as the local mailman. Proud and opinionated, Ernest scorned Sister the first year of her residence in Helvetia, but three years later, the pair decided to marry. The two had been spending evenings at the home of a mutual friend. "Ernest and I would sit in the warm kitchen there and have big arguments—often about women's rights, a moot question at that time," Sister recalled. "He was sure women would never stick together long enough to save the country" (Bourne 1974, 129).

Ernest had contracted tuberculosis, and everyone knew he was living on borrowed time, but she was his first love, and over her family's objections, the pair chose to marry anyway. The family and the community were apprehensive about the teacher's close proximity and prolonged exposure to tuberculosis. When school resumed in the fall of 1919, some of the nervous parents removed their children from school as a precaution.

Sister was distressed by the absences but stuck to her commitment to her ailing husband. One bone-chilling night in the last week of December that year, Eulalia became a widow. The next morning, Sister and a friend loaded Ernest's cold body into the back of his little pickup truck and drove him to Tucson where funeral arrangements could be made. Lacking the money to pay his burial costs, she applied for her first-ever bank loan to pay for the funeral, took two weeks off to mourn, and then returned to school.

Sister remained in Helvetia for four years. However, more and more it was becoming apparent to the young teacher that she would need a university diploma to continue her career. A very supportive county superintendent arranged for Sister to be transferred to a teaching position in Tucson so that she could more easily attend college courses. Eulalia enrolled at the University of Arizona in Tucson in 1920, but it took her ten long years to complete the requirements for her bachelor of arts degree. During this time, she worked her way through college, teaching in the daytime and completing her university courses at night. Finally, she earned her bachelor's degree in letters, arts, and sciences, with a major in English and a minor in Spanish in 1930.

While living in Tucson, Sister taught first grade in a little schoolhouse located on the outskirts of El Barrio Libre, the Yaqui village south of town. The school's two old brick structures were originally used by missionaries as a Presbyterian church. One building housed two classrooms; the principal taught in the larger room, while Sister taught in the smaller one. Later, a storeroom was converted to serve as a third classroom for an additional teacher. That teacher lived with her husband, a missionary preacher, in a rectory about two blocks away. In the second structure, which served as the residence, Eulalia and the principal lived together, an arrangement not entirely to Sister's liking. Eulalia never did appreciate someone looking over her shoulder, in either her professional life or her personal affairs.

At the Barrio school, like the school in Helvetia, the majority of Sister's students were English-language learners, Mexican Americans and Indians from the local Yaqui and Papago tribes. One year, her enrollment included a few Chinese youngsters who had recently immigrated. Eulalia employed all the innovative instructional strategies she developed in Helvetia on this new group of non-English speakers. Her fluent knowledge of Spanish was a tremendous asset when working with the Mexican American and the Yaqui students, but even without speaking their native language, she managed to achieve success with the Papago and Chinese students as well.

During her years in Tucson, Sister married for the third time. The groom was Roy Herman Pennawell, a native of Wellington, Kansas. Of this marriage little is known, except that they were wed on October 16, 1927, and divorced five years later. "My last years in Tucson had been torn by a romance that ended in an impossible marriage that shipwrecked us both," she wrote in her autobiographical account *Ranch Schoolteacher* (Bourne 1974, 164). To escape her painful memories, she accepted the most remote, isolated teaching position she could find. "I had suffered severe emotional damage in my personal life. I wanted to hide far-off by myself to lick my wounds," she confessed (Bourne 1967, Chapter 1). That's how she ended up in Redington, in the San Pedro River Valley of Pima County, seventy-five miles from Tucson, in September of 1930.

While living in Tucson, Sister learned to drive, and she'd acquired a little secondhand Model A Ford which she drove around the picturesque Santa Catalina Mountains through the village of Oracle to her new teaching post. Redington was an accommodation school, an alternative school regulated and maintained by a county superintendent, as opposed to a traditional school district, and it served the children of the residents of the area's massive Carlink Ranch. When she arrived, she was charmed by the quaint little schoolhouse, a small adobe shack located at the top of a mesa overlooking the river road and wooded bottomland.

On the first day of each school year, Eulalia was careful to dress professionally. She appeared in her classroom in a smart new dress, usually a shade of blue to complement her eyes, with heels and hose. But a wardrobe like that was hardly practical for the topography of the Arizona desert, and after the first day, the teacher made it her habit to show up to her classroom in attire more suitable for ranch work: Western shirts, Levi's, cowboy boots, and Stetson hats. This wardrobe became her trademark.

That first year in Redington, the teacher and her students — seven boys and four girls, none of whom could read — created a monthly newspaper of student work entitled *The Little Cowpuncher.* The publications were reproduced on a salvaged mimeograph machine and included lively, detailed descriptions of life on the ranch and in the country school. Each student in the class contributed at least one piece to each issue. They wrote news stories, editorials, book reviews, original stories, poems, riddles, plays, and announcements, and they also created original drawings and cartoons. Single copies were sold for five cents each; yearly subscriptions cost ten cents per month. In later years, the *Arizona*

Daily Star in Tucson reproduced a February edition of *The Little Cowpuncher* in its special annual rodeo edition. The children's work was received so enthusiastically that in 1941 the publication won a Blue Ribbon Award from the Columbia Scholastic Press Association. Today, issues of *The Little Cowpuncher* are viewed as unique historical documents of Southern Arizona ranching communities from 1932 to 1943.

Eulalia also introduced her Carlink Ranch students to the art of making pottery. Together, they dug up the local red soil, strained it through a screen, and mixed it with water to create their clay. After the teacher showed the students how to fashion pots, candleholders, small bowls, or ashtrays shaped like hats, she baked the products in her oven. The next day, the students used watercolors to paint designs on their pieces, and then they applied shellac to seal the colors. The students' creations were given to relatives as gifts or sold at an annual fair to raise money to pay for the supplies needed to produce *The Little Cowpuncher.*

It was while Eulalia was teaching at Redington that the county superintendent met a filmmaker known only as McFarland, who was sent to Eulalia's classroom to make a newsreel of the talented teacher in her one-room country schoolhouse. The filmmaker arrived, accompanied by a woman employed as a feature writer for a Tucson newspaper. The writer authored an article about Eulalia's innovative school projects, and McFarland filmed the students arriving at school on horseback, completing their lessons at their desks as the teacher patrolled the aisles, eating lunch together under a mesquite tree, and creating their pottery pieces. The students published accounts of the filmmaker's visit in their May 25, 1933, issue of *The Little Cowpuncher.*

Throughout the first sixteen years of her teaching career,

Sister had always lived in residences provided by the local school boards. She yearned for the independence of her own home. In her third year of teaching at Redington, she filed papers on a homestead in Arizona's Pepper Sauce Canyon. The property was located above San Manuel, five miles from where the river road crossed the canyon, twelve miles from the nearest town of Oracle, and twelve miles from the school. Eulalia selected this site because it was one of the few available with access to water, a precious commodity in the southwestern desert. With the assistance of an old Texas "mudhen"—a nickname given to a man who managed wells, windmills, and pumps—Sister salvaged some pipes from an abandoned mine, opened up a shallow well in the bottom of the canyon at the foot of a giant cottonwood tree, and installed a water system. His pay for this job was sixty dollars a month and his favorite food, "picked-out pecans," which she delivered to him when she went home each weekend, along with other supplies for the project and whatever necessities the mudhen needed for his cold, soggy campsite (Bourne 1967, Chapter 1).

In the beginning, Eulalia slept in a tent pitched under the thin foliage of a native mesquite tree. It was the middle of the Depression, but on her meager teacher's salary, she was still able to hire some Mexican workers to fire adobe bricks and build the walls of a new house. The structure, which consisted of one room, a bath, a fireplace, and a roof made of new lumber, took five months to complete. Once the cabin was habitable, she slept on a bedroll on newly laid floors of white pine. Later, with help from a hired hand she always called the Old Cowman, Eulalia added an additional room to serve as bunk space for her ranch hands; a barn for her cow horse, Buddy; and some mesquite corrals for her herd, fifty cows she purchased for fifteen dollars a head. Now, not only was Sister a teacher, but she was also a cattle rancher. She was only 5'6" tall and weighed a scant 107 pounds, but she worked as hard as any man on her ranch, her home for the next eighteen and a half years.

Eulalia genuinely enjoyed the three years she spent teaching in Redington's Carlink Ranch school, and she appreciated the independence she gained through living on her own homestead, but, unfortunately, her love life once again had become complicated. "While I was at Redington a three-cornered *affaire d'coeur* began that tormented me and the two men involved for eight, long, anxiety-filled years," Sister confessed. "I was a long time escaping sentimental entanglements" (Bourne 1974, 188). She decided it would be best for all concerned if she moved on.

Sister's next school was Baboquivari, located on the Pozo Nuevo Ranch on the Papago Indian Reservation in the Altar Mountains, fifty miles east of Tucson, just twenty miles from the Mexican border. Baboquivari lay a hundred inconvenient miles south of Eulalia's homestead, and the daily drive over primitive roads was grueling. Despite the hardships, Sister quickly became devoted to the twenty students she inherited at this little country school.

At Baboquivari, Eulalia continued to produce *The Little Cowpuncher* that had generated so much success in Redington. The January 1937, issue revealed excitement among the Baboquivari students, because on Christmas their teacher had received a battery-powered radio from "Mr. Santa Claus." Two students mounted the antenna on the school's roof and another installed the ground-wire tubing. With the device, the youngsters were able to hear President Franklin D. Roosevelt deliver his second inauguration speech and listen to his historic fireside chats. They were also exposed to contemporary music, updates about the Spanish Civil War, and news reports about Howard Hughes' record-setting cross-country flight (Bourne, *The Little Cow-puncher*, Jan. 19, 1937).

During this time, Pima County instituted a nutrition program that made it possible for teachers to serve hot cocoa to under-weight youngsters. Taking advantage of the program for the benefit of her students, Eulalia dutifully weighed each child in her class to determine which youngsters were eligible, and then she carefully recorded the weight gains of each. After a few months, however, the program was suspended and the state initi-ated a lunch program in its place. Fourteen of the youngsters in her classroom qualified for the free lunches. The tender-hearted teacher was unwilling to feed some students in the class and not others, though, and she made sure every student received a cup of cocoa, an orange, and a sandwich every day. To accomplish this, Eulalia added weekly trips to the grocery store to her already burdensome list of tasks and enlisted the aid of the students to help prepare the snacks and lunches. When the funding for the program was cut off, the teacher continued to provide the snacks and lunches by paying for the groceries out of her own pocket (Bourne 1969, 207–209).

Every year in early spring, Eulalia escorted her Baboquivari students on an excursion to the Tucson Rodeo. The annual event was basically a cowboy reunion, which featured daredevil com-petitions in riding, roping, and horse racing. Invariably, the chil-dren's favorite events were the clowns, the trick riding, and the parade. The rodeo of 1937 was particularly memorable because that was the year that the Baboquivari students produced their award-winning float depicting the cowboy lunch under the ramada.

The rodeo of 1937 was also the year that Sister's students staged an impromptu choir performance in the lobby of the Santa Rita Hotel on the night before the big annual Fiesta De Los Vaqueros (Cowboy Festival). The audience was composed primarily of hotel guests, cattle ranchers, and rodeo people. After securing permission from the hotel manager, the children stepped onto the tiled floor of the hotel lobby dressed in their well-worn and oft-patched Western clothes. One of the kids toted an old guitar which he strummed for accompaniment. The Baboquivari children were full of natural talent, possessing pleasing voices and the ability to harmonize well. Sister taught them a repertoire of ranch songs and Mexican melodies, mostly ballads. "Spontaneously, Mexican fashion, they sang full blast with simple harmonies curiously effective. Even the smallest knew the words and sang them out," Eulalia later described. "There were wild yells from the cowboys scattered among the audience, and gay shouts of approval from all sides. We were a hit" (Bourne 1969, 131). By the third song, the spectators began to shower the youngsters with coins. A total of $14.85 was collected that night, which was later divided evenly among the children, seventy-five cents apiece, a veritable fortune for the impoverished kids.

Years later, in retrospect, Eulalia expressed regret for taking her students to the annual rodeo. She recognized that these field trips were an educational project that gave the students an opportunity to experience a world beyond the limited environs of Pozo Nuevo Ranch, but the teacher nevertheless acknowledged that the violent nature of rodeo sports generated a cruelty toward animals that, philosophically, she found in her later years she simply could not support (Bourne 1974, 201–204).

During the Baboquivari years, Sister married again. This fourth husband was Jack Ryland, a local cowpuncher. True to form, she reveals little detail about this union in her autobiographical works. It is known, though, that Jack owned the homestead a few miles below her Pepper Sauce Canyon ranch, and that when this marriage dissolved, his property became annexed to hers.

After five fulfilling years at Baboquivari, most of Sister's students had grown up and graduated, and in 1939, the school was closed. The teacher accepted her next job offer from Sasco in Pinal County, forty miles from Tucson. This country school was located on the ranch of J. C. Kinney, the long-time sponsor of the little cowpunchers at Baboquivari. About twenty eager, well-behaved students who worked on Kinney's ranch or a neighboring one, attended the Sasco school. All the children spoke English, and all but three of them spoke Spanish. To the teacher's relief, she found that most of them could already read.

Sister found her teacher's quarters less delightful, however. She was assigned two ramshackle adobe rooms, about a block from the stables and corrals and about two blocks from the schoolhouse. The dilapidated structure boasted no modern conveniences, not even an outhouse. Water was carried into the house in buckets filled from a spigot around the corner of the building. The place was swarming with mice, scorpions, cockroaches, and flies. Faced with this disagreeable dwelling, Sister opted to rent a room in Tucson for fifteen dollars a month, which meant a grueling round-trip drive of eighty miles every day.

She also returned to her Pepper Sauce Canyon homestead

every weekend. Although the United States had not yet officially entered World War II, the country was gearing up for the conflict. Essentials such as tires and auto parts became difficult to obtain, and prices on other goods were rising fast. Expenses to keep the Pepper Sauce ranch solvent often outstripped Eulalia's meager income, so she moonlighted by keeping books for some local livestock investors. While the investors raked in a tidy profit, Sister garnered merely fifty cents an hour and her dinner. Eventually the investors moved their livestock herds to Flagstaff, and Sister lost her second job. By this time, the daily grind was wearing on Sister's health. She had to find a better-paying job closer to home.

Sister's next teaching position was at Sasabe, about half a mile from the border with Mexico. Located in Pima County, this little country school was nestled in the Altar Valley, surrounded by tall, picturesque mountains and rolling green hills. The area was named Sasabe, a Papago Indian word meaning "echo," because the hills were so hollow that when a person shouted, an answering echo could be heard. Nearby was the famous historic guest ranch known as Rancho de la Osa. In its heyday, this remote dude ranch hosted such distinguished visitors as Presidents Franklin D. Roosevelt and Lyndon B. Johnson, western novelist Zane Grey, and Hollywood celebrities John Wayne and Tom Mix. Dick Jenkins, the owner of Rancho de la Osa, was also the clerk of the board at Sasabe. He often encouraged the children of his guests to attend Eulalia's school while they were vacationing at his ranch. Rose Mary Thurber, the daughter of writer James Thurber, and Bill Mellon, one of the children from the well-known Mellon family of Pennsylvania, were among these temporary dude ranch students (Bourne 1974, 231). Permanent

140

students included the children of La Osa ranch hands and several Mexican nationals who walked across the border to attend.

After only one year, declining enrollment at Sasabe necessitated another change of employment. This time, Sister found a post in the one-room schoolhouse at Sopori, only forty-five miles from Tucson. In Sopori, as in all the rural schools where Eulalia taught, she carried with her an arsenal of tried-and-true lesson plans, including the homemade songbooks (but not the dancing), the "memory gems," the outdoor play (baseball had become the national sport), pottery making, *The Little Cowpuncher*, and the annual expedition to the Tucson Rodeo.

While Sister was teaching at Sopori, the United States entered World War II in response to the bombing of Pearl Harbor on December 7, 1941. Eulalia remembered the day well. She was on her ranch in Pepper Sauce Canyon, putting a fried chicken dinner on the table for her three ranch hands, when her portable radio broadcast the news. At school the next day, the teacher and her students created an issue of *The Little Cowpuncher* that revealed the children's thoughts and anxieties about their country's sudden and unexpected involvement in the war. The effort proved to be therapeutic for all (Bourne 1974, 237-238).

One year, during the annual excursion to the Tucson Rodeo, the heroic teacher saved the life of one of her little charges. The Sopori students, including five-year-old Lee Bell, were getting their float ready for that year's entry in the rodeo parade. They watched the teamsters hitch their horses to their wagon; nearby, another float was assembled, as a huge ore wagon was hitched to a team of two half-broken horses. One of the horses was a sorrel Clydesdale marked with a long white streak on his face; the other was a dapple gray Percheron that was so wild it took several men to harness him. As the participants waited for the signal to begin the parade, Sister and her students shivered in the cold, drizzly morning and huddled around a makeshift street fire for warmth. Suddenly, the Percheron bolted, pulling the Clydesdale with him. The driver couldn't control the two frenetic horses as they dashed down the street, jumped the sidewalk, and galloped directly toward Sister's children. When the kids saw what was coming, they scattered for dear life, all except little Lee, who was paralyzed with terror and couldn't move a muscle. Horrified onlookers screamed in panic, fearing that the enormous horses and the massive wagon trailing behind them would trample the defenseless child. In split-second timing, the teacher dashed between the frantic horses and under them, grabbing the little girl and shielding her with her own body. Over the pair and down the street thundered the horses and the wagon. After they were gone, Eulalia pulled Lee up into a sitting position and examined her for injuries. Both had sustained superficial cuts to their scalps where the Clydesdale's huge hooves had grazed their heads, and a sharp bolt from under the wagon had ripped the teacher's blouse and scraped the skin from two of her ribs, but otherwise, remarkably, the pair escaped major harm (Bourne 1974, 240–243).

After only one year in Sopori, Sister returned to her former post at the Sasabe school but found the conditions more difficult to endure than her previous stint there. World War II was still in full swing. Dick Jenkins had closed his dude ranch at Rancho de la Osa to accept a commission in the United States Air Force, eliminating the financial support and encouragement Sister enjoyed before. And then there was the arduous 125-mile round-trip drive from Sasabe to her ranch in Pepper Sauce Canyon. Nevertheless, Sister persevered.

A week before the opening of school in September 1943, Eulalia was badly injured when she was thrown from a bucking horse. She was hospitalized in Tucson. It was December before she was able to return to her school, and even then, she was on crutches. In her absence, her substitute teacher had accepted too many students from the other side of the border. Mexican nationals were required to pay a monthly tuition of two dollars, the equivalent of twelve pesos of Mexican money, which few could afford. Luisa Escalante, the acting clerk of the board, instructed Eulalia to collect the tuition or send the extra students away. Unable to cast out any of the needy youngsters, the soft-hearted teacher paid their tuition for them, calling her donations a "scholarship."

Sister taught for two years at Sasabe until, once again, she decided she needed to find a position closer to home. She spent the final eight years of her long teaching career at the little country school on the McGee Ranch at Sierrita, Pima County, on the western rim of the Santa Cruz River Valley, forty miles from Tucson. She was specifically recruited for this school, whose under-performing students were in desperate need of remediation. They were a restless bunch, poor but proud, and full of misdirected energy. "They were clean and adequately clothed. But the school atmosphere was not good," recalled Eulalia. "They were not involved. They were clock-watchers, without even a clock to watch," she described (Bourne 1974, 259). Once again, the teacher rolled up her sleeves, rearranged the desks, lugged in her portable phonograph and radio, and filled the blackboards with lessons, outlines, and memory gems. Just about every student was behind in grade level, and Eulalia was especially concerned for the two eighth grade boys who were required to pass their achievement tests in order to move on to the high school. With Sister's expert teaching, however, both boys passed their tests and earned their promotion.

Eulalia officially retired from the teaching profession in 1957, after forty-three years of challenging work. A few years following her retirement, she traded her ranch in Pepper Sauce Canyon for a similar property in the Galiuro Mountains in an agreement with the Magma Copper Company. Her new ranch, which she christened the GF Bar Ranch, was located in the rugged terrain east of the San Pedro River, six miles down a rough dirt road on Copper Creek. There she lived a relatively primitive lifestyle; she had no phone, no mail delivery, and no electricity. She used firewood for heat and a gas-powered generator for her lights and television. She was isolated there, but she was content.

During her retirement years, Eulalia wrote three books about her teaching career and ranching experiences: *Woman in Levi's* (1967), *Nine Months is a Year at Baboquivari School* (1968), and *Ranch Schoolteacher* (1974). One year, a fire destroyed her home, which she rebuilt. Unfortunately she lost many mementos and treasures from her teaching career that she had collected over the years. However, she was able to donate surviving issues of *The Little Cowpuncher*, with their hand-drawn illustrations, to the Special Collections Room of her alma mater, the University of Arizona in Tucson. These have been digitalized and are accessible online.

During her long career, Eulalia Bourne received accolades and recognition for her work in Arizona country schools, including awards from the University of Arizona Alumni Association, the organization Arizona Press Women, and the Arizona Library

Association. She was also inducted into the Cowgirl Hall of Fame. Although she married four times, Sister never had any children of her own. During her retirement years, she maintained a correspondence with almost fifty of her former students until the early 1980s, when severe arthritis in her hands made it impossible for her to write. She died at about age ninety of natural causes on May 1, 1984, at her GF Bar Ranch, and she was buried in Oracle Cemetery in Oracle, Pinal County, Arizona. Eulalia always remembered with fondness her long and remarkable career in country schools. "If I ever come back in a second life," she once said, "I hope I'm a teacher."

Educator Leonard Covello was an innovator of community-centered education and a promoter of cultural pluralism, seen here in September, 1953. Photo by Ralph Morse/Time Life Pictures/Getty Images.

8

LEONARD COVELLO
He Was an Innovator of Cultural Pluralism

*The most extraordinary thing about a really
good teacher is that he or she transcends
accepted educational methods.*
MARGARET MEAD

A young Leonard Covello and his buddy, Vito Salvatore, trudged dutifully along New York's Second Avenue in the direction of 115th Street, keeping pace with Leonard's father, who marched purposefully ahead leading Leonard's two younger brothers by their hands. Nine-year-old Leonard, newly arrived in the United States, had replaced his long European trousers with the short knickers that were in fashion at the time, and he wore black-ribbed stockings and brand new American shoes. To the people he passed on the cobbled street, Leonard appeared to be an average American kid, except he could not speak one word of English.

Leonard was born on November 26, 1887, in the southern village of Avigliano, in the mountainous Basilicata region located at the instep of the boot of Italy. In 1890, when Leonard was only three years old, his father, Pietro Covello, immigrated alone to

New York City. Six long years later, Leonard, his mother, and his two brothers followed Pietro to America, and the reunited family settled in a tenement flat near the East River at 112th Street in East Harlem, which at that time was an enclave of Italian immigrants. Despite the reunification with his father, and despite living within an Italian American community, Leonard, nicknamed Narduccio, was a lonely, homesick little boy. He found himself suddenly thrust into bewildering new surroundings, he missed the familiar terrain and fresh air of his mountain home in Italy, he found his own father a stranger, and he missed the Italian uncles who had become his father surrogates.

Almost immediately following Leonard's arrival in America, his father enrolled him in La Soupa Scuola, a "soup school" organized and sponsored by the Female Guardian Society of America, a Protestant mission. In those days, the primary purpose of a soup school was to "Americanize" newly arrived immigrants, equip them with a functional understanding of English, and familiarize them with the customs and practices common to their new environment.

"The Soup School got its name from the fact that at noontime a bowl of soup was served to us with some white, soft bread that made better spitballs than eating in comparison with the substantial and solid homemade bread to which I was accustomed," Leonard recounted in his autobiography. "Why we went to the Soup School instead of the regular elementary public school I have not the faintest idea, except that possibly the first Aviglianese to arrive in New York sent his child there and everyone else followed suit and also possibly because in those days a bowl of soup was a bowl of soup," he continued (Covello and D'Agostino 1958, 22–27). Located at 116th Street and Second Avenue, the

Soupa Scuola was a three-storied wooden building flanked by two five-storied tenements. To Narduccio, the building seemed huge and intimidating when compared to the shabby, ill-equipped one-room village school he had attended back in Avigliano.

In many ways, La Soupa Scuola was not that much different from the village school Narduccio attended in Avigliano. Leonard's parents raised their children in a very strict manner, and Leonard found this same strictness was the major characteristic of the first of his American schools. His biggest surprise was the presence of women teachers, but he soon discovered that a smack from Mrs. Cutter, the soup school's middle-aged, gray-haired, stockily built teacher, did not possess quite as much sting as one from Don Salvatore Mecca, his village teacher in Avigliano. In both places, the prevailing philosophy was "the student must suffer to learn" (Perrone 1998, 81).

In the soup school, the young immigrant studied English, grammar, spelling, arithmetic, US geography, and penmanship. He was interested in his lessons and endeavored to be a diligent student, but he found the teaching strategies, typical of the period, uninspiring. Leonard remembers that every lesson was infused with rote memorization. "You recited to the teacher standing at attention. Chorus work. Repetition. Repetition until the things you learned beat in your brain even at night when you were falling asleep," recalled Leonard (Perrone 1998, 88). This rote memorization and repetition was bewildering to the young immigrant who was desperately looking for some meaning attached to his lessons.

After two years, Narduccio's scholastic progress in the soup school was advanced enough that he could transfer to the local public school. He completed his elementary education at New York's Public School 83, located on 110th Street between

Second and Third Avenues. The economic progress of the family, however, was not as successful. In the Old Country, Leonard's father had worked at shoemaking and upholstering, but like most Italian immigrants living in East Harlem, Pietro could only find jobs as an unskilled laborer. He was employed intermittently as a general handyman in a German tavern on Twenty-Second Street. During the winter, he earned a meager seven to eight dollars per week plus tips; in the summer, business usually slowed significantly, and Pietro was often laid off for weeks at a time. Winter or summer, there was never enough money, and the Covello family, which now included four sons and another child on the way, lived in a perpetual state of poverty.

In those days, it was typical in Italian immigrant families for the parents to place greater emphasis on working than on studying, and male children were expected to contribute financially to the household income as soon as they possibly could, sometimes when they were as young as five or six. To meet this parental expectation, Narduccio got a job delivering baked goods for the nearby bakery located at 112th St. and Fifth Avenue. He was only twelve years old and considered short and scrawny for his age, but the shopkeeper hired him anyway. Leonard's parents were happy and proud. "Good," Pietro praised his oldest son. "You are becoming a man now. You have grown up" (Perrone 1998, 93).

Once he started working, Narduccio's life became a ritual of rising at 4:30 each morning, enduring the bitter cold to make his deliveries, and then, because he was committed to continuing his education, a full day at school. He worked six days a week for a salary of $1.75 per week and a cup of coffee with a roll each morning. After school, Narduccio would return to his family's shabby tenement apartment to scrub the floors, wash the windows, and watch his little brothers. After that, he did his homework. It was a difficult childhood, but Narduccio was proud of himself because, "I could earn money and stand on my own two feet and help keep the family together, as I had been taught practically from the time I was born was my responsibility" (Perrone 1998, 93).

In 1902, Leonard transferred to Morris High School, the first high school built in South Bronx. Leonard and his buddies were perplexed to find the facility coeducational. It was a custom in old-school Italian families to separate the girls and the boys, practically from infancy. Italian immigrant boys were not accustomed to associating with girls, and they found the situation unsettling.

Another aspect of high school life that Leonard found difficult to understand was the enormous emphasis placed on sports. He had been raised to believe that play, even for youngsters, was a frivolous waste of time and energy. Despite his initial reluctance to participate, Leonard desperately wanted to be accepted by his peers, and it soon became obvious that he was a talented athlete. He was designated captain of Morris High School's senior basketball team, and he played the position of halfback on the city championship soccer team in 1906. To his surprise, Leonard excelled well enough to earn a letterman sweater, despite the fact that he received no support for this accomplishment at home.

In spite of his athletic achievements and his academic successes, by the end of Leonard's third year of high school, the pressures of family and poverty overruled his love of school. His after-school earnings were not enough to contribute significantly to the family, so he decided to drop out and work full time. His father worked, so did his two younger brothers, but still the family could not make ends meet. His parents did not question his decision to quit school. Leonard got a job loading and unloading crates six days a week for a company that manufactured brass-ware on Murray Street in downtown Manhattan. The pay was five dollars a week. The money helped to ease things financially at home, but not enough to make the sacrifice worth it, Leonard thought. After a year, he decided to return to Morris High School and earn his diploma. "I wanted to go to school," confessed Leonard in his autobiography. "School meant books and reading and an escape from the world of drudgery which dulled the mind and wore out the body and brought meager returns" (Perrone 1998, 95). To replace the income lost when he gave up his full-time job, Leonard gave English lessons to Italian immigrants at home, charging fifteen to twenty-five cents a session.

While in his last year of high school, Leonard began to think about his life after graduation. He fervently wanted to go to college, but given his family's financial circumstances, he abandoned all hope this would ever be possible. However, with the assistance of his English teacher, Leonard applied for and was granted a prestigious Pulitzer scholarship that enabled him to enroll in Columbia University. The scholarship covered his college tuition and provided an annual income of $250 to cover his living expenses (Johanek and Puckett 2007, 83).

Leonard was thrilled at the prospect of attending college, but his happiness was tempered by his mother's poor health. The Covello matriarch had never adjusted well to life in America, and she languished from a severe and prolonged depression. By the time Leonard entered high school, he could see that she was very ill. "Many times she would just sit with her hands folded in her lap, an air of weariness upon her," Leonard recorded in *The Heart*

Is the Teacher. "She lost all desire to go out into the street, as if just keeping alive was problem enough in itself" (Perrone 1998, 96). During Leonard's senior year, the doctor confirmed their worst fears: her illness was terminal. In the summer of 1907, she died, just before Leonard began his coursework at Columbia University.

Leonard attended the Morningside Heights campus of Columbia from 1907 to 1911, completing courses in romance languages with a major in French. During these years, Leonard supplemented the family income by teaching English to Italian immigrants two nights a week at the Aguilar Library nearby. By the time he graduated from college, Phi Beta Kappa, he decided that his future career would be in teaching.

In 1914, Leonard was hired to teach French at DeWitt Clinton High School, an all-boys school located in Manhattan on Tenth Avenue between Fifty-Eighth and Fifty-Ninth Streets, a neighborhood dubbed Hell's Kitchen. Described as an academic school, DeWitt Clinton enjoyed a reputation for academic rigor, but before long, Leonard noticed some troubling trends among his Italian American students: their attendance records were abysmally poor, and their dropout rates were appallingly high. Those who did attend school regularly generally performed significantly lower than their ability levels. Leonard's personal experiences as an Italian immigrant made it possible for him to clearly understand the contributing factors behind these trends.

Leonard recognized that for a variety of social and economic reasons, the majority of Italian immigrant parents felt apprehensive about educating their children, and they opposed sending their offspring to school beyond the elementary grades. These parents perceived the American educational system to be a threat to the family, because they believed that if their children became more educated or more successful than themselves, the parents' status as role models and authority figures would be diminished. The result, they predicted, would be the disintegration of the family, the only institution the parents believed had any real value. As recent arrivals from a society in which social interaction between the classes was minimal and intermarriage was unthinkable, the concept of upward mobility for their children was unwelcome. "The school takes our children away from us," Italian immigrant parents frequently complained (Meyer, n.d., "Leonard Covello: Cultural Pluralism"). Furthermore, Italian immigrant parents depended on their children to work and make a contribution to the household income at the earliest age possible. Even when the family's economic situation improved, strongly negative feelings about education persisted. Italian immigrant students often found themselves conflicted, because they recognized that very often, their success in school required that they reject the values of their culture, abandon their native language, negate their relationships with their parents, and impose an economic hardship on their families.

To ease these conflicts, Leonard began to develop an innovative instructional program he called "community-centered education." The focal point of his vision was a close partnership between the school and the community; the school would energetically reach out to the community, while the community would become intimately involved with the school. According to Leonard's plan, community-centered education included three essential components. The first component was the introduction of classes in the Italian language to be added to the instructional program at DeWitt Clinton High School. Leonard believed that the Italian language was an important bridge between the young people and their parents, and that recognition of a community's first language was an important sign of respect. The second component was to establish student clubs called Il Circolo Italiani, which would offer opportunities for its members, primarily Italian American students, to participate in community service projects, recreational pursuits, and cultural activities. These clubs would provide opportunities for students and their parents to explore and celebrate their Italian culture. The third component would be the founding of the Casa del Popolo, a settlement house located in Italian Harlem. This institution would offer food, shelter, citizenship classes, and educational opportunities to all the members of the community. The settlement house would be financed by the charitable donations of wealthy sponsors, and it would be staffed by student, teacher, and parent volunteers who would all be working together to accomplish shared goals.

Leonard's extensive agenda for community-centered education was moving ahead strongly when, suddenly and without warning, historic events in Europe intervened. On June 28, 1914, the heir to the throne of Austria-Hungary, Archduke Franz Ferdinand of Austria, was assassinated by a Yugoslav nationalist. A month later, on July 28, the empire of Austria-Hungary invaded Serbia, triggering the outbreak of World War I.

A week later, in August of 1914, Leonard married his childhood friend and confidante Mary Accurso, whom he had known since his earliest days in America. The Accurso family had emigrated from the same hometown in southern Italy as the Covellos. Leonard's father had boarded with the Accursos while he raised the money to pay for the passages of his wife and children so they could join him in New York. It was the Accurso matriarch, Carmela, who readied the tenement flat and arranged the welcome party with relatives and friends to greet them on their arrival. Leonard and Mary grew up together, and Mary helped Leonard become acclimated to American life. When they were teenagers, she frequently served as a bridge between Leonard and his parents, softening the tensions between the generations and helping Leonard to cope. Without Mary, it is unlikely that Leonard would ever have attended college, for it was she who encouraged him to consider the possibility, and it was she who urged him to apply for the Pulitzer scholarship which financed his undergraduate studies at Columbia. Like Leonard, Mary became an educator, teaching at PS 191 in lower Manhattan. Sadly, she developed a severe case of nephritis and passed away, after just one short year of marriage (Johanek and Puckett 2007, 86).

During World War I, in the summer of 1917, Leonard contributed to the war effort by volunteering to direct the Farm Cadet Bureau, an employment program for high school students sponsored by the Committee on War Service and organized by the board of education in Milton, New York. Because so many young men had been called to war, the state's fruit and berry industry was experiencing a critical shortage of manual labor, and the Farm Cadet Bureau sought to fill that void.

Leonard believed this contribution was not enough, however, so on December 10, 1917, he enlisted as a private in the United States Army Fifty-Seventh Artillery Corps, Battery D; he was stationed at Fort Hancock in Sandy Hook, New Jersey. He felt compelled to go, primarily as a show of support and respect for his students from DeWitt Clinton High School, many of whom had also enlisted. When Leonard reported for boot camp, he found himself training side-by-side with many of his former students (Perrone 1988, 15).

Following basic training, Leonard was stationed in the south of France, where the Italian-born American soldier worked as an interpreter. In the summer of 1918, he was promoted to the rank of sergeant and transferred to the Corps of Intelligence Police in Hendaye to serve as a linguist. On military orders, the thirty-year-old sergeant crossed the border between France and Spain on a mission to gather information about German activity in Spain, which was then a neutral country. Leonard became so fluent in Spanish that he was able to pass for a native speaker. He spent nearly a year traveling throughout Spain, following leads and sending intelligence reports back to his base in Paris (Johanek and Puckett 2007, 89).

Following the Allied victory in WWI, Leonard, now an American veteran, accepted a job at an international advertising firm based in New York City lining up advertisers with South American markets. In this position, the financial rewards were greater than those he had ever known as a teacher. He was given a swanky office located midtown on Fifth Avenue, but Leonard found the work tedious and mind-numbing. After a year, he happily returned to his former teaching post at DeWitt Clinton High School. Not long after his reinstatement, Leonard courted and then married Mary Accurso's younger sister, Rose. The newlyweds rented a small apartment near New York University, and Rose quit her job as a secretary at an export company in order to complete her education. She also wanted to go into the teaching profession.

Immediately upon his return to DeWitt Clinton, Leonard picked up where he left off in the development of the community-centered education programs he was organizing prior to the war. He finally succeeded in his goal to add classes in the Italian language to the high school curriculum. Lacking a decent textbook for beginning Italian, Leonard and a colleague, Annita Giacobbe, authored one, but the poor scholastic performance of the all-boys school's Italian students was still a cause for concern. Before long, Leonard's principal designated Leonard as the head of a counseling program for at-risk students. Leonard, who was affectionately known as "Pop" to the boys, organized afternoon sessions in peer tutoring and made frequent home visits to ask parents to encourage their sons to do well in their studies. He also established an active Italian Parents Association. Leonard consistently communicated the concept that "the unit of education was not merely the child. The unit of education must be the family" (Covello and D'Agostino 1958, 158).

Always thinking of more ways to connect the school and the Italian community, Leonard organized additional projects. From 1921 to 1926, he published *Il Foro,* a literary and cultural magazine in both Italian and English, which featured student essays and articles written by leading Italian American scholars. With his students, Leonard raised funds to purchase books in the Italian language for the school library. Also, he recruited former DeWitt Clinton students to teach English to Italian parents, conduct citizenship classes, volunteer as leaders of East Harlem boys clubs, and participate in the recreational and cultural activities sponsored by Il Circolo Italiani.

By 1931, Leonard could see a need for a new school facility located geographically closer to the community he was serving. From 1931 to 1934, he campaigned vigorously to establish an all-boys high school in East Harlem. The indefatigable teacher envisioned an expansion of the community-centered instructional programs he had set in place at DeWitt Clinton. "What was in the back of my mind," recorded Leonard in his autobiography, "was a neighborhood school which would be the educational, civic, and social center of the community. We wanted to go beyond the traditional subject-centered and the current child-centered school to the community-centered school" (Johanek and Puckett 2007, 111). As a result of his effort, in September 1934, East Harlem's Benjamin Franklin High School opened with an enrollment of two thousand boys, and Leonard Covello served as the school's first principal.

One feature that was unique to Benjamin Franklin High School was the establishment of what Leonard called "street units." Street units housed recreation, research, and educational activities that encouraged community members, business owners, parents, teachers, and students to work collaboratively to improve the quality of life in their neighborhood. The street units were located in refurbished store fronts on the same block of East 108th Street as Franklin High's main building. The high school also offered a children's day school, an afternoon community playground for neighborhood youngsters, and an evening community center for adults. Students from the school organized a community cleanup and beautification campaign. In fact, the school was open and in use twenty-four hours a day, seven days a week. Under Leonard's pioneering leadership, this innovative and progressive school was one of the first urban community schools, offering programs that emphasized the movement of cultural pluralism, recognized the special needs of immigrant students, promoted full racial equality, and presented a model for integrated education.

Leonard was also involved in numerous activities outside of Benjamin Franklin High School. Besides his educational and administrative work in the New York City school system, he also taught courses at several colleges and universities in the New York metropolitan area. He taught courses in the French, Spanish, and Italian languages, Italian culture, and educational theory. The most important courses he taught, however, were on the community-centered school and the social background of the Italian American student at New York University's School of Education.

Leonard also started work on his doctorate. In 1944, he earned his PhD from the School of Education at New York University. After devoting forty-five years of his life as a dedicated teacher and visionary administrator, Leonard retired in 1956. He was sixty-nine years old, but he still had more service to offer. He became an educational consultant for the Migration Division of the Puerto Rican Department of Labor. Leonard understood that, like the Italian immigrant students of his youth, the educational needs of Puerto Rican students had been woefully neglected. He worked indefatigably on developing language and literacy campaigns, citizenship programs, conferences and workshops on Puerto Rican problems, and raising awareness and pride in Puerto Rican history and culture. He worked for the Migrant Division until 1968. During this period, Leonard was also instrumental in the founding of the American Italian Historical Association.

He was eighty-five years old in 1972 when he returned to his native Italy. His second wife, Rose, had passed away by then, and the couple had never had any children. While in Italy, Leonard continued his work as a social activist. He devoted the last ten years of his life to community projects at the Center for Study and Action, founded by Danilo Dolci, an Italian social reformer, sociologist, and educator.

Leonard Covello died at the age of ninety-five on August 19, 1982, in Messina, Italy. In his obituary, the *New York Times* heralded him as one of the greatest educators in the history of New York City. His entire career was a model for inspirational teaching, for showing how the community can be successfully connected to the school, and for demonstrating how the school could be productively employed as an instrument for positive social change. The cultural pluralism for which he was such a strong advocate is still evident in the wide range of programs that appeal to cultural diversity, which can be found in present-day public classrooms. "I believe and will always believe in the potential in every boy to lead a good and useful life—if we as adults will only care enough, take the time and the trouble and the expense to develop his potential," asserted Leonard in his autobiography *The Heart Is the Teacher*. "The teacher is the heart of the educational process and he must be given the opportunity to teach—to devote himself wholeheartedly to his job under the best circumstances. Half a century as a teacher leads me to the conclusion that the battle for a better world will be won or lost in our schools" (Perrone 1998, 144).

Leonard Covello's life story was the embodiment of the American dream: he came to this country a poverty-stricken immigrant, but through perseverance, self-determination, hard work, and education, he became a man of noteworthy success.

Educator Gladys Brandt, champion of Native Hawaiian culture, assists
students at the Kamehameha School for Girls in Oahu, Hawaii. 1963.
Used with permission from Kamehameha Schools, Copyright 2001
Kamehameha Schools.

9

GLADYS KAMAKAKUOKALANI BRANDT
She Taught Native Hawaiians

A teacher affects eternity;
he can never tell where his influence stops.
HENRY B. ADAMS

Shortly before the start of the 1966 Kamehameha Schools Song Contest, a distinguished-looking woman of Native Hawaiian descent entered the auditorium at Neal Blaisdell Center in downtown Honolulu. She was unusually tall and lean, with bright eyes framed in wide-rimmed glasses. She had a thin and elongated face; a broad smile revealing straight, white teeth and dimples in her cheeks; a nose wide and prominent; a high forehead; and long, dark hair that she had pinned neatly into a twist at the back. A light sweater over her shoulders covered a crisply starched blouse; her heeled pumps and handbag perfectly matched the color of her straight-lined skirt. A gold wristwatch, a string of pearls, and clip-on ear rings completed her ensemble. The woman was Gladys Kamakakuokalani Brandt, principal of the Kamehameha School for Girls, and she had come to watch her students compete in this highly anticipated annual event.

163

Gladys was particularly interested in the standing hula competition, newly introduced that year after a long and bitter battle with school administrators. The smile on Gladys's face expanded as she observed the graceful performances of the barefoot students dressed in traditional attire, a hibiscus flower tucked behind the left ear of each girl to signal her status as a single woman. Gladys thrilled at this renaissance of Native Hawaiian culture represented by the time-honored songs and dances presented in the competition. This achievement, Gladys mused, was worth the battle, no matter which group of students won the trophy.

The competition's origins were far-reaching, going back forty-five years. The Kamehameha School for Boys' first song contest was held as a tribute to George Alanson Andrus, a beloved music teacher who suddenly collapsed and died on May 26, 1921. That same day, as a tribute to Andrus, the principal and the faculty hastily organized an impromptu choral competition between the classes. That first event was held in the dark on the steps of the campus's Bishop Museum, illuminated only by the headlights of automobiles aimed at the contestants. The following year, the Kamehameha School for Girls staged their first annual song contest. Beginning in 1952, the competition combined the boys' and the girls' groups. Each year, the coveted Andrus Trophy was awarded to the winning choral group.

In the early days of the contest, each class sang the school's alma mater, "Sons of Hawaii," followed by a Hawaiian composition, and culminating with an original song in Hawaiian composed by members of the class. Even though under ordinary circumstances the students were not allowed to speak in their native Hawaiian, the language was permitted for the purposes of the contest. In 1968, the popular competition was televised for the first time, live, with a simulcast on radio. Today, the event is still highly anticipated, and, like the very first competition, the song selections are still delivered a cappella. The students spend many weeks in preparation for the program, and participation is mandatory for students graduating from the school's Kapalama campus.

Kamehameha Schools are among the most prestigious in Hawaii; they derive from a long and illustrious history that dated back to the late nineteenth century, when the islands were first colonized by missionaries from the mainland. Contact with the world outside the islands had expanded, and Hawaiian chieftains believed it was essential to educate the future rulers of the kingdom in Western ways. They established a school for the royal children and recruited teachers from nearby Protestant churches whose missionaries had converted many of them to Christianity. A well-liked and competent married couple from New England, Amos Starr Cooke and Juliette Montague Cooke, were placed in charge of the new school.

One of the royal offspring who attended the Chiefs' Children's School was Princess Bernice Pauahi. A favorite at the school, she was well-behaved, dutiful, and industrious. An intelligent youngster, she quickly learned to read and write in English. She loved books and in her teens served as the school's librarian. In addition, she possessed remarkable musical talent, playing the piano expertly and singing in a pleasing contralto voice. Pauahi grew up to be a beautiful young woman, slender and graceful, with fair skin and long, dark hair that fell in ringlets to her waist. She was known for her exceptionally beautiful hands.

When she came of age, Pauahi married an American, Charles Reed Bishop, although this union was against her parents' wishes. They had selected another royal child attending the Chiefs' Children's School, Prince Lot, to be her husband, and eagerly looked forward to a state wedding. The princess resisted the match, for she had already fallen in love with Charles. Born in New York, Charles immigrated to Hawaii in 1846 and worked as the collector of customs. Even though he was a "haole," a foreigner of Caucasian descent, he was highly respected in the Hawaiian community. Unlike the princess's parents, the Cookes were delighted by Pauahi's marriage to Charles, believing him to be a worthy choice for the princess. In addition, Pauahi was the last remaining royal child living at the school, and her departure paved the way for the Cookes to close the facility and move on to other interests (King and Roth 2006, 18–19).

The marriage between Charles Bishop and Princess Pauahi was a long and happy one, but to the couple's sorrow, they had no children. Their union lasted thirty-four years, until Pauahi died of breast cancer on October 16, 1884, at the age of fifty-two. By the time of her death, Princess Pauahi had become an important and powerful Hawaiian "alii," an individual of chieftain status. She was adored and respected by the Hawaiian people, and the entire kingdom mourned her passing. She was interred in a formal state burial at the Royal Mausoleum in Mauna Ala, Honolulu, which was the final resting place for members of the Kamehameha and Kalakaua Dynasties.

At the time of her death, Pauahi was an extremely wealthy woman. Her lands and other assets had an estimated value of more than half a million dollars, which over the decades developed into a financial behemoth. She was always deeply devoted to her people, and she left explicit directions in her will that two schools, one for boys and one for girls, be built and maintained expressly for the purpose of educating Native Hawaiians. These schools, which would serve both day students and boarding students, were to be called Kamehameha Schools. Princess Pauahi emphasized her goal that underprivileged Hawaiian children would be formed into "good and industrious men and women." Vocational training and academic study would be provided, along with moral and religious instruction (King and Roth 2006, 32). She further designated a panel of five trustees to administer her trust, which for many years after was referred to as the Bishop Estate.

In accordance with the princess's will, the Kamehameha School for Boys opened with great fanfare on November 4, 1887, with thirty-nine students. The campus encompassed a sprawling six hundred acres in Kapalama Heights on the main island of Oahu, spread over the verdant hills overlooking Honolulu Harbor. William Brewster Oleson, a Protestant minister, was selected as the first principal. The opening of the Kamehameha School for Girls followed in 1894 with thirty-five students. The girls' school was located across the street from the boys' campus. Ida May Pope, a Protestant missionary, was selected as the first principal. In 1889, the Bernice P. Bishop Museum, which chronicles Native Hawaiian history, and a memorial chapel for worship were also established on the grounds.

It was at the Kapalama campus that Gladys Kamakakuokalani Kanuha was born on August 20, 1906, when Hawaii was still an American territory. At the time of Gladys's birth, her parents lived at the school. Her mother, Esther Staines Kanuha, was a favorite of Ida Pope and a member of the first graduating class of Kamehameha School for Girls. Gladys's father, David Kanuha, was the first, and for many years the only, Native Hawaiian member of the faculty of Kamehameha's Manual School for Boys. Beginning June 27, 1893, he taught a vocational course in tailoring. In fact, the students in David's classes crafted all their own shirts, all the uniforms worn at Kamehameha Schools, and the teachers' suits.

Before Gladys's birth, David's teaching career had been briefly interrupted when he became involved in a counter-revolutionary movement determined to restore the monarchy of the Hawaiian queen, Liliuokalani, whose reign had been overthrown with the assistance of the United States government in a nonviolent coup in 1893. The ill-fated insurgence was led by royalist Robert William Wilcox in 1895; it lasted a mere three days. When arms were found in the gardens of the Queen's residence, she was placed under house arrest and finally forced to renounce her throne (Daws 1968, 282–283). David Kanuha was dismissed from his teaching position at the school, arrested, and convicted of treason for his role in the plot. He spent only a few days in jail, however, and reinstated, he returned to the campus to resume teaching. Despite his conviction and incarceration, Native Hawaiians considered David a hero, and they later elected him to the new territorial legislature. He did not entirely abandon his rebellious fervor, however. When Gladys was sixteen, he changed the family's last name from Kanuha to Ainoa, which in Hawaiian means "to eat in freedom," a reference to a rallying cry when the cultural restrictions against men and women eating together were lifted.

Gladys was the fifth-born child, the first daughter after four brothers. According to custom, her parents gave her a Christian first name, followed by a Hawaiian name. David and Esther named their baby daughter Gladys because, she once said, "they were glad to have me." In honor of her maternal grandmother, they gave her the Hawaiian name Kamakakuokalani, which means "the upright eyes of Heaven," an allusion to the divine imagination of an artist (Apgar 2003).

According to tradition, any Hawaiian child, whether the child of a chieftain or a commoner, could be claimed and brought up by relatives or close friends of the birth parents. This practice was called "hanai." At the age of four, Gladys became the hanai daughter of Ida Pope, who had become a very close friend of Esther. David and Esther felt the haole upbringing Ida could provide would be to their young daughter's advantage. "My father and mother, like virtually all Hawaiians at that time, wanted their children to succeed, and they believed that to do so required their children to adopt Western ways. Unfortunately, they thought this was possible only by leaving behind the Hawaiian language and culture," Gladys once remarked (Eyre 2004). Perhaps this explains why, as a child, Gladys rejected Hawaiian customs, spurned the Hawaiian language, and rubbed her skin with lemon juice in an attempt to lighten it.

Gladys's hanai mother, Ida Pope, had immigrated to Hawaii in 1892 from her hometown of Columbus, Ohio. She had a reputation for being devout, strong-minded, and exacting. Her expectations for both her staff and her students were extraordinarily high. The teachers she hired for the girls' school were all, like herself, single women from the Midwest. They were generally better qualified than the men teachers at the boys' school, and they stayed longer at their teaching posts than the men did, even though their salaries were lower. Under Ida's guidance, the academic performance and knowledge of English of the girls far exceeded that of the boys and the dropout rate of the girls was considerably lower (King and Roth 2006, 38).

A multilevel wooden structure located at King Street and Makua Street served as the first school building for the girls. Ground level rooms included an administration office, an assembly hall, classrooms, a gymnasium, and a dining room. At the rear of the structure were the kitchen, a scullery, the pantry, and a storeroom. The second story rooms served as dormitories for teachers and students. A sewing room, a music room, an equipment room, and the matron's room were also located on the upper level. The basement housed the area designated for laundry and ironing.

Life at the girls' school was highly regimented. The students would rise at 6:00 a.m. every morning. They washed their faces, brushed their teeth, made their beds, and swept and dusted their rooms. At 7:00 a.m., a bell rang to summon the faculty and children to breakfast, where Ida offered a short and simple prayer of thanksgiving. Breakfast was followed by a devotional period for both faculty and students, which included a lecture about religion, life, or manners. On Sundays the girls dressed in crisp, white dresses and long, black stockings and marched across the street to the Bishop Memorial Church for services. Sunday evenings were spent reading the will of Princess Pauahi or discussing the life of their benefactress. On Mondays the girls did their laundry, on Thursdays they did their ironing, and on Saturdays, they got down on their hands and knees and scrubbed the floors (*Makers of Destiny* 1981, 184–185). On weekday mornings the students attended classes in academic subjects, they received vocational training in the afternoons, and daily physical education was mandatory.

Although Ida was strong on discipline, she was beloved by her Kamehameha students. The girls often referred to their principal as "Mother Pope" or "Mama Pope." Gladys once confessed that she was very spoiled by Ida, and that as a child she "was not the most well-behaved creature on earth" (Ishikawa and Creamer 2003). Gladys enjoyed her life as Ida's hanai daughter until Ida's sudden death in the summer of 1914, when Gladys was only eight years old.

In 1917, when she was only eleven, Gladys was one of the privileged few to attend the funeral of Queen Liliuokalani, the last reigning monarch of the Hawaiian Islands. Liliuokalani's death on November 11 was announced by the somber tolling of bells and the flying of flags at half mast. The former queen had been educated with Princess Pauahi at Kamehameha School when it was known as the Chiefs' Children's School, so the royal red and yellow feathered capes, considered national treasures, were stored at the Bishop Museum. So, too, were the royal kahili, ten-foot poles inlaid with tortoise shells bearing fan-shaped rows of sacred feathers from the "mamo" and "oo" birds, which are rare species that nest in high, rocky places that are dangerous for climbers. The queen's body originally lay in state at historic Kawaiahao Church, a house of worship founded by Protestant missionaries, but after seven days of mourning, an elaborate state funeral was held in her former throne room at Iolani Palace. Following the ceremony, her casket was borne in a dignified and elaborate procession to her final resting place in the Royal Mausoleum at Mauna Ala, near the burial site of her hanai sister, Princess Pauahi.

A few years after the passing of Ida Pope, young Gladys became unhappy at Kamehameha. She persuaded her father to let her leave the boarding school and return to the home of her parents, who were by then living in their own residence in Honolulu. Gladys was transferred to public school, enrolling first at Robert Louis Stevenson Intermediate, and later moving up to President McKinley High School, where she graduated in 1925.

After graduation, Gladys enrolled in the teaching program at Territorial Normal and Training School, located on the slopes of Punchbowl at Lunalilo and Quarry Streets in Honolulu. This teacher training school is now connected to the University of Hawaii, Manoa Valley. Two years after beginning her teaching training program, in 1927, Gladys completed the requirements to earn her teaching certificate.

Although highly respected by those who knew her, Gladys often described herself as a self-centered young woman, appreciating nothing and feeling responsibility to no one. According to Gladys, that all changed during her student teaching year. One day the regular teacher failed to show up for class. "Gladys stepped to the front of the room," recounted colleague Randall Roth. "As she turned around and looked at the students, she said she almost fell to her knees when she saw all those innocent little eyes looking squarely at her, trusting her totally. Gladys resolved then and there never again to be so unworthy" (Roth 2008).

Following her graduation from Territorial Normal, Gladys married Isaac Kaleialoha Brandt in Honolulu on August 6, 1927.

Isaac's father, Hermann, emigrated from Germany to Hawaii in 1882, where he met and married Isaac's mother, Lily, who was a Native Hawaiian. Isaac was born on August 25, 1905, in Koloa, Kauai, the sixth of seven children born to the German Hawaiian couple. The union of Gladys and Isaac produced two daughters, Esther Lillian, born in 1928, and Lorita Gladys, born in 1930.

Early in her professional career, Gladys became a classroom teacher in the one-room schoolhouse in the sleepy little village of Keanae on Maui, an island known for its tropical rainforest. Keanae is situated on the rocky northern shore near Wailua, halfway between Paia and Hana. The students in Gladys's classroom came from low-income families that cultivated small plots of taro, an indigenous root vegetable used to make poi, a staple in the Native Hawaiian diet. These families also fed themselves with fish and fruit from clumps of banana trees, which grew in abundance in the area. Like student populations throughout the Hawaiian Islands, Maui children represented many cultures, including Native Hawaiians, Chinese, Japanese, Filipinos, Koreans, Portuguese, and Spanish. These children came from immigrant families recruited to work in the sugar plantations and pineapple fields. Dealing with so many different languages and cultures in one room must have been particularly challenging for the territory's teachers, but Gladys wholly embraced the motto of her alma mater, the University of Hawaii, "Above all nations is humanity."

It was during Gladys's first year of teaching that a book rental system was instituted throughout the Hawaiian Islands. Previously, students bought their own textbooks, which was a financial burden for many families, as most were living on limited incomes. In addition to the book rental system, some districts were served by a bookmobile that made regular visits, providing a selection of library books and an eagerly anticipated story hour. Eventually, territorial schools were equipped with a complete library staffed with full-time library personnel.

After leaving Maui, Gladys accepted a teaching position in a grammar school in the little village of Eleele, located near Hanapepe Bay on the south shore of the island of Kauai. The island is famous for its white sand beaches, crystal clear blue waters, and natural plantations. The curriculum in Kauai's grammar schools was similar to that used throughout the islands; it included instruction in the English language, phonics, reading, arithmetic, penmanship, geography, crafts, art, gardening, and folk dancing. But there were no limitations placed on class size, and Kauai's teachers often were required to cope with as many as sixty-five youngsters in one class.

Gladys was a veteran teacher with fourteen years of experience when the Empire of Japan bombed Pearl Harbor on the island of Oahu on Sunday, December 7, 1941. Residents throughout the Hawaiian Territory, including teachers, were taken by complete surprise by the attack. Schools were closed immediately and martial law was declared. Nevertheless, the next day, teachers in Honolulu reported to their school sites to set up first aid stations, drive ambulances, and help care for women and children survivors from Pearl Harbor and Hickam Field. Temporary shelters were set up in schools until displaced families could be placed in more permanent homes (*Makers of Destiny* 1981, 33). Then word came that the army ordered all school facilities evacuated within one week, so teachers went to work clearing out student desks, instructional materials, textbooks, and other supplies. Classrooms were relocated to anywhere else where there was space—churches, theaters, storefronts, and empty buildings. When the government ordered every person on the islands to be enumerated and fingerprinted, teachers were pressed into service to complete these tasks.

In February, classes resumed. To help with the war effort, teachers organized air raid drills, developed evacuation plans for their communities, and volunteered to issue ration cards. Gas masks were issued, and school children were taught how to use them. In some districts, teachers and high school students worked side-by-side in the sugar cane fields to cultivate and harvest crops that would otherwise have been abandoned because of a shortage of labor. After a period of about five months, school buildings were returned to the teachers by the army, which had found other quarters. At the end of that difficult and demanding year, during commencement exercises at schools, such as Kamehameha and Gladys's alma mater, McKinley High, each graduate carried his or her own gas mask through the ceremony (*Makers of Destiny* 1981, 89).

Despite the disruption to normal life caused by the events of World War II, 1943 saw Gladys complete the requirements for her bachelor's of education degree from the University of Hawaii, Manoa.

In the late 1940s, Gladys returned to Kauai to accept a position at Kapaa High School. The school was located on a coconut tree-covered bluff known as Mailihuna Hill, which commanded a magnificent view of the Pacific Ocean. Established in 1883 during the reign of King David Kalakaua, the school graduated sixty-six seniors in 1946. While in Kapaa, Gladys forged a reputation as "an absolute firebrand in the best sense of the word," recalled Waimea Williams, the daughter of a teacher who worked with Gladys.

"Kapaa was soon too small for this courageous woman and she moved to Honolulu to champion advanced education for Hawaiians. This meant tackling the most entrenched prejudices of her time" (Williams 2004, 119). The perception that Native Hawaiians were unfit for any work other than manual labor was common among the haole population, and Gladys sought to correct this faulty belief. By 1962, Gladys became the first woman in Hawaii to serve as a district superintendent of schools.

The following year brought a new challenge for Gladys. In 1963, she became the first individual of Hawaiian descent to become the principal of her former school, Kamehameha School for Girls, and in 1969, when the boys' and girls' schools were combined, Gladys was promoted to director for the high school division.

Like Ida Pope before her, Gladys had a reputation for being strict, hardheaded, and strong-willed, but she was highly respected because she used these traits to better the lives of the people around her. "The stories I've heard when she was principal here, she was a real hard nose, but she was fair," former Kamehameha Schools President Mike Chun once commented. "When I talk to kids who had gone to school then, they have a lot of aloha for her" (Daws and Kamehameha 2009, 38).

Gladys always believed her position as an educational leader and a role model was very important for her students. "I wanted them to witness a Hawaiian in a leadership position, so that they would know that as a group we were not all born to be followers," she said in a 1986 keynote speech at a convocation ceremony that commemorated the hundred-year anniversary of Kamehameha Schools. "I wanted them to see a Hawaiian take on weighty responsibilities so that they might become more confident in assuming such challenges for themselves. I wanted them to share in another Hawaiian's success so that they would realize that this is our right and our potential," she expounded (Brandt 1986).

In the 1960s, Gladys had a dramatic change of heart regarding her Hawaiian roots, no longer rejecting them, but rather, embracing her Native Hawaiian culture. One of the most important accomplishments Gladys achieved in her years at Kamehameha Schools was to persuade Bishop Estate administrators to rescind the deeply entrenched taboo against the standing hula. Missionaries had long before outlawed the traditional dance, believing it to be a pagan practice and sexually suggestive. However, in many countries around the world, folkloric dancing was considered a cultural asset, and many Native Hawaiians believed the same respect should be accorded to the hula. Gladys set about convincing her supervisors, the five Bishop Estate trustees, that the ethnic dances should be allowed. She was able to use her powers of persuasion to convince the first four men, but the fifth trustee proved more difficult. Her conference with the administrator was nothing short of a debacle. When the puritanical man accused Gladys of promoting indecency, Gladys lost her temper, yelling at her superior and dissolving into bitter tears. Believing she would surely be fired for her audacity, she returned to the campus and began to pack her bags. To her astonishment, the executive later phoned her office and somewhat angrily agreed to lift the ban on the hula (King and Roth 2006, 58).

After Gladys regained her composure, she immediately hired Nona Beamer to teach classes in Native Hawaiian language, culture, and dance to Kamehameha's girls. Ironically, in the 1940s, while a young student at Kamehameha, Nona was expelled for performing a standing hula at a tea party hosted by Bishop Estate trustees. Only when her grandmother pleaded on her behalf did the trustees reconsider and reinstate her. Since 1928, Nona had been teaching hula during school vacations at her mother's Waikiki dance studio, counting among her apprentices such Hollywood celebrities as Mary Pickford, Shirley Temple, and Dinah Shore (Rath 2006, 80–81). As a young woman, Nona won a scholarship to Colorado Women's College, and later she was given a Guggenheim Fellowship which paid her tuition at Barnard College, an institution then associated with Columbia University. Over the decades, Nona's extensive knowledge and skill in chant and dance caused her to be regarded as an authority on Native Hawaiian traditions and a highly respected cultural icon. It was Nona who first coined the term "Hawaiiana" to refer to Native Hawaiian history and culture. For Gladys, Nona Beamer was the ideal choice to lend an air of respectability to her new Hawaiian culture program.

For her part, Nona returned the admiration. According to Nona, Gladys was the perfect example of a modern, Westernized, Hawaiian woman, always dressed to the nines, with matching hats, gloves, shoes, and purses. Gary Obrecht, a Kamehameha Schools Secondary English teacher, agreed. "I always saw her as very regal and set apart, and yet she was very down to earth. A beautiful combination of earthiness and kind of being set aside. An alii (leadership) quality in a contemporary setting. Very dignified," Gary recalled. "Even as a young woman she had class. Not just in how she dressed. She carried herself and treated people well. She was always one individual, and you could trust she would be that individual. Integrity," he concluded (Daws and Kamehameha 2009, 38).

Gladys worked at Kamehameha Schools for eight years, and then retired in 1971 after a forty-four-year career as an educator. She continued to maintain a close association with Kamehameha Schools even after her retirement, especially during a crisis period in the 1990s that rocked the institution to its core. With four other highly respected community leaders, Gladys coauthored and published an essay entitled "Broken Trust" which generated a criminal investigation into dubious business practices by Bishop Estate trustees. The inquiry resulted in the eventual removal of all five trustees, although only four of them were blameworthy, and led to sweeping reforms at the schools. "I did not enjoy my role as critic, but I felt I had little choice," Gladys once confessed. "The resulting turmoil was painful but necessary" (King and Roth 2006, xi).

Following her retirement, Gladys continued to lend her expertise to educational endeavors. She served on the board of the Aha Punana Leo Hawaiian Immersion Program and was instrumental in shaping the University of Hawaii's Center for Hawaiian Studies, which was later renamed the Kamakakuokalani Center for Hawaiian Studies in her honor. In 1981, Gladys was given an honorary doctorate of humane letters by the University of Hawaii. From 1983 to 1989, she was appointed by Hawaii Governor George Ariyoshi to the Board of Regents for the University of Hawaii, serving four years as the chairperson. In 2000, the University of Hawaii Alumni Association recognized Gladys with a Lifetime Achievement Award.

As a cancer survivor of thirty years, Gladys also served on the boards of Wilcox Memorial Hospital, Kapiolani Children's Medical Center, and the Cancer Center of Hawaii. For her many years of service to the community, Gladys was recognized with the Juliette Award for National Women of Distinction from the Girl Scouts, USA, and the same year, the West Honolulu Rotary Club honored her with the David Malo Award, given for her efforts in perpetuating Hawaiian culture. In 1985, the Honpa Hongwanji Mission of Hawaii bestowed upon her their prestigious Living Treasure Award.

Gladys's husband, Isaac Brandt, died on July 19, 1992, and was buried in Koloa Cemetery in Koloa, Kauai. He was eighty-six years old. Gladys followed him a little more than a decade later. She passed away from natural causes on January 15, 2003, at Queen's Medical Center in Honolulu, Hawaii. She was ninety-six. Following observances held first at Kamehameha Schools Chapel and then at University of Hawaii's Kamakakuokalani Center, her funeral was held on January 29 at Kawaiahoao Church, the same church where Queen Liliuokalani, Hawaii's last monarch, lay in state seventy-five years earlier. Mourners, including descendants of royalty, governors, judges, teachers, former students, and admirers, filed past Gladys's lei-draped portrait and the urn that contained her ashes. Her burial was celebrated with twenty-four hours of traditional chants, prayers, and ancient rituals dating back to the funeral of Queen Liliuokalani. Many of the women dressed in traditional white muumuus (loose-fitting Hawaiian dresses). Because Gladys was descended from the ancient, high-ranking chiefs of Kalanipouu, attendants dressed in regal red and gold capes and wearing white gloves flourished white-feathered kahili, the symbol of an alii, a person of chieftain status (Apgar 2003). The elaborate Hawaiian ceremonies were followed by a simple Christian service. All over the state, flags were flown at half mast in her honor.

Throughout her long career, Gladys was an extraordinary educator, a champion for Native Hawaiian culture, and an exemplary role model for leadership, especially during times of conflict. "In education, not anger, resides our future," Gladys once asserted. "In education, not ignorance, resides our hope. In education, not fear, resides justice" (Apgar 2003).

Teacher Mary Tsukamoto (back row, third from left) with family and friends in front of barracks, block 9, at Jerome Relocation Camp in Jerome, Arkansas, during WWII. 1944. Photo courtesy of California State University, Sacramento.

10

MARY TSUKAMOTO
She Developed Internment Camp Programs

*The most creative and emotionally engaged teachers
see themselves not just as educating learners and
workers, but as developing citizens.*
ANDY HARGREAVES AND MICHAEL FULLAN

On a peaceful Sunday morning at the beginning of the Christmas season of 1941, Mary Tsukamoto was among the jovial worshippers attending the weekly service in their local house of worship, the Methodist church. As Christmas lights within the church twinkled cheerfully, the building resonated with a merry rendition of "Joy to the World." Suddenly the church door burst open, and Mary's husband, Al, rushed in, noticeably shocked and visibly frightened. "Pearl Harbor has just been bombed!" he shouted to the people assembled in the church. "I just heard it on the radio. We are at war with Japan!" (Tsukamoto and Pinkerton 1988, 16). The Japanese immigrants and their American-born children paused in stunned silence. They, too, were noticeably shocked and visibly frightened. The members of this close-knit community of Florin, California, were well acquainted with the sting of bald-faced anti-Asian prejudice and the patent discrimination of anti-Asian laws. What would happen to them all, wondered Mary, now that the land of their birth was at war with the land of their ancestors? A quiet panic ruled the room.

Mary Tsuruko Dakuzaku was born on January 17, 1915, in San Francisco, California. She was the third child born to her parents, Taro and Kame Yoshinaga Dakuzaku, who had immigrated to the United States from Okinawa, Japan. When they immigrated, the couple left behind a seven-year-old daughter, Masaka, to care for her grandmother. In America, the Dakuzakus enlarged their family with the birth of their second daughter, Ruth, in 1913. In addition to Masaka, Ruth, and Mary, three more daughters and a son were born to the couple: Isabel, in 1917; Jean, in 1920; Julia, in 1922; and their only son, George, in 1925. As immigrants from Japan, Taro and Kame were known as Issei, first generation. Their children born in America were known as Nisei, second generation.

When Mary was ten years old, the Dakuzakus closed their family business, a laundry in San Francisco, and relocated to Florin, California, a little town nestled in the Sacramento Valley at the foot of the snow-capped Sierra Nevada Mountains. Florin, settled primarily by Japanese immigrants, was a small and cohesive agricultural community. The area was known for its berry fields, orchards, and vineyards. Mary's parents, like their neighbors, produced strawberries and grapes on the thirty-five-acre farm that they worked. Legally, the farm belonged to Mary's older sister, Ruth. Because her parents had been born in Japan, they were not allowed to own land in California, according to the Webb-Haney Act, the state's anti-alien land law, which was passed in 1913. Children born in the United States could own land, so the

Dakuzaku family farm was purchased in the name of their oldest American-born child.

Issei parents were typically very committed to providing the best educational opportunities possible for their children, so at his earliest opportunity, Taro enrolled his children in Florin Grammar School. He was taken aback to discover the school was segregated, with an entirely Japanese student body and an entirely Caucasian faculty—the community's Caucasian students attended the new brick school built down the road—but he was determined that his children should succeed to the best of their ability in their new school.

Mary possessed an extraordinarily positive outlook on life and quickly adjusted to her new environment, despite a pervasive anti-Japanese prejudice. She soon settled into a routine of school, church, and work on the farm. As a ten-year-old, Mary had long, thin legs and a long neck. Her Japanese name, Tsuruko, means "stork," and her family often teased her by saying that she resembled the skinny, long-legged bird (Tsukamoto and Pinkerton 1988, 45). Mary enjoyed school immensely. She got along well with her teachers and earned high grades.

When Mary was old enough for high school, in the fall of 1929, she transferred to Elk Grove Union High School. During her four years at Elk Grove, Mary was greatly influenced by one special teacher, Mrs. Mable Barron, who taught courses in public speaking, drama, and English literature. One spring, Mrs. Barron assigned her students to prepare a speech about the life of a distinguished Californian. The speeches would be performed in an oratorical contest sponsored by the Native Sons of the Golden West. For her topic, Mary selected John Muir, a prominent environmentalist and conservationist. Mary was a shy and reluctant public speaker, so she was surprised and excited to learn that she had been selected as one of the nine finalists. Her pleasure quickly turned to disappointment, however, when she was disqualified because contest rules did not allow participation by the children of immigrants. Mrs. Barron was incensed by the discrimination but powerless to change the rules. A short time later, with Mrs. Barron's assistance, Mary entered an oratorical contest sponsored by the Sacramento Junior College Students' Club. As a result of Mrs. Barron's expert coaching, Mary garnered first prize. By the time Mary graduated in 1933, she had entered many more oratorical competitions and essay contests, always finishing near the top, and two years in a row she earned a medal for being the top scholar in her class.

After Mary's graduation from Elk Grove High, she aspired to become a teacher but resigned herself to full-time work on the family farm. After all, the Depression was in full swing. With limited means, Taro and Kame could afford to send only one child to college, and that honor was reserved for Mary's older sister, Ruth. Mrs. Barron, however, had other ideas. Secretly she arranged for Mary's admission to her own alma mater, the College of the Pacific (COP), in nearby Stockton, California. She secured a $150 scholarship to pay a portion of Mary's tuition, persuaded fellow teacher Mrs. Helen Householder to contribute ten dollars per month toward expenses, and convinced Taro to allow his daughter to attend the college. Then she fashioned a wardrobe for the young coed by altering a selection of secondhand clothes. In the fall of 1933, the grateful farmer's daughter was ready to begin her coursework at COP.

Mary flourished at COP, a private university affiliated with the United Methodist Church. One of the oldest chartered universities in California, the institution offered a church-centered curriculum that was well-suited to Mary's temperament. As she strolled the leafy campus among the picturesque brick-faced buildings, past the Gothic-style music conservatory, or through the celebrated rose garden, the shy, self-effacing young woman felt warmly welcomed and deeply appreciative of the opportunity to study in an atmosphere free from racial prejudice (Tsukamoto and Pinkerton 1988, 68).

However, despite her scholarship money and the generous gifts of Mrs. Barron and Mrs. Householder, Mary faced a continuous struggle to raise the rest of her tuition money. After her first semester, Mary enrolled in a student work program. Every day she swept, mopped, and dusted classrooms. On weekends, breaks, and summer vacations, she washed windows and cleaned dormitories. Although grateful for the work, Mary developed a debilitating case of rheumatoid arthritis, and the physical demands of the job caused severe inflammation of her joints. In her junior year, the condition forced her to quit school and return to her family in Florin.

Throughout her college years, Mary had dated her high school sweetheart, Iwao Alfred Tsukamoto, known to everyone as Al. The popular and handsome suitor had been a star halfback on the high school varsity football team and also played on the baseball and basketball teams. Mary was twenty-one years old when the couple married on November 22, 1936. The newlyweds moved into the farm home of Al's parents, Kuzo and Ito Kadokawa Tsukamoto. The next year, on April 7, 1937, their only child was born, a daughter they named Marielle Bliss.

Al and Mary settled into the routine of married life, which included working on the Tsukamoto farm, tending acres of grapevines and fields of strawberries and boysenberries. The numerous vines and plants needed constant cultivation, which involved planting, weeding, hoeing, irrigating, and fertilizing. It required dawn-to-dusk stooping, crawling, bending, and picking. This work was physically taxing for Mary, who still suffered from painful bouts of arthritis. To make ends meet, Al took a job with the Florin Fruit Growers Association. Both became active in the local chapter of the Japanese American Citizens League (JACL). Founded in 1929 and still operational, JACL is an organization dedicated to promoting the educational, cultural, and social values of the Japanese American community. Al and Mary became active in their church, Florin Methodist, where Mary taught a weekly Sunday school class. The couple was not wealthy in monetary terms, but they were active, joyful, and contented.

That is, until December 7, 1941, which President Franklin D. Roosevelt declared a "day that will live in infamy." Pearl Harbor, Hawaii, was attacked by the Empire of Japan. United States military forces were taken completely by surprise, and much of America's Pacific Fleet was destroyed. A total of eighteen naval ships were sunk or severely damaged, and 188 aircrafts were flattened. To the nation's sorrow, 2,402 servicemen and civilians were killed, and 1,282 were wounded. The following day, in an emotional address to the stunned nation, President Roosevelt declared war on Japan and its allies, the Axis Powers.

A wave of hysteria followed the attack and declaration of war, resulting in the issuance of Executive Order 9066 on February 19, 1942, which authorized the Secretary of War to order the roundup of individuals of Japanese ancestry, who might be involved in espionage, and their relocation to detention camps away from the Pacific Coast. The order applied even if they were United

States citizens. Of the over 120,000 such individuals living in Washington, Oregon, California, and Hawaii, seventy thousand were American citizens. Authorities appeared to be particularly distrustful of Japanese Americans who had attended Japanese language schools, private schools that stressed a curriculum of Japanese language, culture, and customs. These organizations were financially supported by parents who were concerned about the loss of their native traditions and the increasing Americanization of their children.

Under the authority of Executive Order 9066, sixteen specific locations throughout the state of California—places such as race tracks, fairgrounds, and labor camps—were converted into makeshift detention facilities to accommodate the internees until more permanent relocation sites could be constructed. General John L. DeWitt, Commander of Western Defense Command, ordered the entire Japanese American community in Florin to prepare for evacuation from the West Coast, which was declared a "zone of exclusion." In response, in April 1942, Mary was appointed the Executive Secretary for the Florin chapter of the Japanese American Citizens League (JACL). In this capacity, Mary worked with the US Army, the Wartime Civil Control Administration, the Federal Reserve Bank, the Farm Security Agency, and social welfare workers to ensure the needs of evacuees from Florin were adequately met. She coordinated the collection of clothing, toiletries, food, and other supplies for the mass departure. During this time, Mary was also busy with patriotic duties, such as writing letters to Nisei soldiers, completing a first-aid class, rolling bandages, and organizing a local Red Cross group.

The next month, Mary, her husband, Al, and their five-year-old daughter, Marielle, were ordered to report to the Elk Grove train station for evacuation on May 29, 1942. A similar order was issued to her in-laws, Kuzo and Ito Tsukamoto, and her husband's younger sister, Namiyo, known as Nami, who had been diagnosed with tuberculosis and had been undergoing treatment for three years. These six Tsukamotos learned that their family number was 22076. Also evacuated were members of Mary's Dakuzaku family, including her parents, Taro and Kame Dakuzaku, her sisters Ruth, Isabel, Jean, and Julia, and her teenaged brother George. After boarding the train, the Tsukamotos, the Dakuzakus, and other members of Florin's Japanese American community bid goodbye to their freedom and began their long journey toward incarceration.

Later that day, the train pulled into the station at Fresno Fairgrounds in rural Fresno County, California, which had been hastily set up as an assembly center. There in the dry, barren desert stood row after row of unsightly, black, tar-paper covered barracks surrounded by a barbed-wire fence. A uniformed military guard carrying a rifle surveyed the new arrivals from a tall watchtower equipped with a powerful searchlight. Most of the barracks became primitive housing for over five thousand internees, while some were designated for use as a mess hall, a laundry, a shower room, and latrines. The center included a total of a hundred barracks–six sets of communal buildings and four blocks of twenty barracks each.

The barracks buildings, many of which had formerly been horse stalls, had been hurriedly converted into living quarters for the internees. Each family was assigned to a one-room portion measuring approximately twenty by twenty-five feet. Floors of new asphalt had been poured, and in the desert heat the tar-like substance, still soft, exuded a strong, unpleasant odor. The walls were constructed of a cheap grade of knotty pine, with knotholes and gaps between the boards so wide that occupants could make eye contact with individuals on the other side. Even the softest whispers could be heard between the partitions. The unfinished ceilings revealed a roughly finished roof of wooden beams with a tar-paper covering. Into this cramped space squeezed the six members of the Tsukamoto family: Al, Kuzo, Ito, Nami, Mary, and little Marielle.

Because of the sudden evacuations, the educational activities of the 1,200 students living in the assembly center had been abruptly interrupted. Parents were anxious to fill their children's idle hours with structure and constructive activity. Within a month of their arrival, the internees organized their own summer school under the capable direction of Inez Nagai, a former physical education teacher at Edison Junior High School in Fresno. Classrooms were formed from any available space where shade could be found—sheds, unfinished shower rooms, laundry rooms, along the shady sides of buildings, and under what few trees were available. The classrooms were unfurnished, and there were no books or teaching materials. Any internee who had completed at least one year of college was recruited to teach in the summer school. A total of thirty teachers were found to work in the relocation camp school, and each was paid by the government a standard wage of sixteen dollars per month. Camp residents also established a nursery school, managed by Senior Girl Scouts who were earning credit toward their leadership training, and supervised by Nisei who had been Girl Scouts in their younger years.

Even the elderly Issei internees attended summer school classes. Mary volunteered to teach them a course in basic English.

"More than 250 enrolled, their wrinkled faces radiant, their eyes bright," remembered Mary. "Long ago, they had sacrificed their personal longings so that their children might be able to be educated, but now it was their turn. They sat on the edges of their seats, eager not to miss a thing," she recalled (Tsukamoto and Pinkerton 1988, 94–95).

In addition to her basic English class, Inez persuaded Mary to teach a course in public speaking for high school students. Mary wrote to her long-time mentor, Mable Barron, and other former teachers to ask them for assistance with lesson planning. Before long, she received letters and packages filled with helpful curriculum resources, teaching tips, and instructional materials. Mary spent the summer session instructing the twenty students enrolled in her class how to overcome their timidity, how to improve their voices and diction, and how to polish their delivery in a way that would command respect and attention.

At the end of July, the summer school's culminating activity was an elaborate display of student work, coupled with a community program of music, drama, and public speaking. The contribution of Mary's class in public speaking was a group recitation of President Abraham Lincoln's *Gettysburg Address*, a choice which caused some controversy, given the circumstances. Mary defended the selection. "We, who were trapped in this camp, needed to remember Lincoln's great words as we searched for some bright thread of hope for our future," she argued. "We had to believe that 'we the people' meant us too" (Tsukamoto and Pinkerton 1988, 97). For the 142 seniors from forty-two high schools who had missed their commencement exercises, a special graduation ceremony was organized, and high school diplomas were presented.

Florin's evacuees spent five long, hot, months in the Assembly Center in Fresno. Just when they began to feel somewhat settled and organized, they were ordered to prepare for another move, this time to their permanent relocation camps. On October 14, 1942, most of the Assembly Center residents were designated to be transported to Jerome Wartime Internment Camp in Arkansas. Clutching small bundles of provisions, these nervous internees were loaded onto ten trains. Four days later, the nearly five thousand passengers, nervous and exhausted, finally reached their destination.

Jerome Camp was situated in Drew County, Arkansas, on the flat, marshy delta of the Mississippi River flood plain. The 10,054-acre property, located between the Big and the Crooked Bayous, was tax delinquent land acutely in need of clearing, drainage, and development (AETN 2010). The area abounded in cypress and white oak trees, persimmon, and lowland shrubs.

The camp was divided into fourteen residential blocks, and in each block, approximately three hundred people were housed. One structure was designated to contain a mess hall, where communal meals were served; another became a recreational building; a third was used as a laundry, and yet another was equipped with latrines and tubs of water for bathing and brushing teeth. Each block was composed of twelve barracks. Each barrack held four to six units measuring approximately twenty feet by twenty-five feet, and each unit housed one entire family. Like the barracks in Fresno, Jerome's barracks were plywood structures covered with tar-paper, which provided little protection against temperature extremes, and there was no running water. Mary's family occupied Block 9, Barrack 8, Unit E. In tall military towers built on stilts and equipped with strong searchlights, armed guards presided over the swampy compound, which was surrounded by barbed wire.

A few months after the arrival of internees at Jerome, educational activities were resumed. Denson High School was opened in January 1943, set up in one of the barracks on the far edge of the camp, a taxing distance to walk for many students. The building wasn't heated in the piercing cold of winter or air conditioned in the searing heat of summer. The principal and most of the teachers were Caucasian, but eighteen of the forty-three teachers were Nisei. Camp teachers were paid a civil service salary of two thousand dollars per year, nearly triple the amount they would have earned in a public school (Takemoto 2006, 134). Typical high school subjects meeting state guidelines were offered, including courses in English literature, algebra, chemistry, physics, and Latin. Equipment and textbooks were in short supply, but a few of the books were the same as those used in regular public schools, and a few were actually brand new. Music instruction was also available. Despite a lack of instruments, the school mustered a nineteen-member band and a fourteen-member orchestra under the direction of music teacher Mr. Robert Head. Piano lessons were offered for school credit, using a piano trucked in and placed in one of the mess halls, originally for use during church services. Classes in physical education were available, as were organized sports such as basketball and baseball, with Nisei coaches. Under the school colors of black and gold, Denson varsity teams competed against high school teams from Rohwer Relocation Camp (Takemoto 2006, 135).

Two elementary schools, the North Side School and the South Side School, served the younger students. Mary's daughter, Marielle, was enrolled in the first grade classroom in Block 23,

Barrack 5. "The wooden floor was bare; a pot belly stove in the middle of the room was surrounded by benches, and that was all there was," recalled Mary. "Cheerfully, though, I smiled for the sake of the children and met the teachers. They looked confident and capable, and they were smiling. That was a good sign," she described (Tsukamoto and Pinkerton 1988, 167).

By 1943, most of the internees had resigned themselves to their incarceration for the duration of the war and had settled into a routine. Then the government decided it needed more soldiers. Their search for new recruits brought them to the war relocation camps. To ascertain who might be the best candidates for enlistment, the government decided to administer a loyalty questionnaire to all interned Japanese American citizens who were seventeen years of age and older. This loyalty questionnaire contained two questions that generated a great deal of controversy and division among the internees. Question 27 asked if the responder would be willing to serve in the armed forces of the United States on combat duty, wherever ordered. Question 28 asked, in part, if the individual would be willing to swear unqualified allegiance to the United States, and renounce any form of allegiance to the Emperor of Japan. Many internees found these questions distressing. They feared if they answered "no, no," this could result in accusations of disloyalty to America and immediate deportation to Japan. Many were so angry about the internment of themselves and their loved that they refused to fight for the United States on principle. On the other hand, a "yes, yes" response could be interpreted as a previous allegiance to Japan, and they worried that if the United States lost the war, they might lose potential citizenship in Japan as well, leaving them stateless. Some internees attempted to answer yes, yes on the condition that conditions at the camps would be improved or closed down completely (Dudley 2002, 18–19).

Bitter debates about the appropriate or necessary responses and the potential consequences to these loyalty questions raged in nearly every family's quarters. "Battles continued between children and their parents ... between those who chose patriotic loyalty to their country rather than filial loyalty to their aged parents," Mary remembers. "Little apartments were far too small for the battles that waged in almost every room. Young people and old were stunned and dazed from the daily verbal assault," she described (Tsukamoto and Pinkerton 1988, 148). The Tsukamotos, however, were spared such family quarrels; they were in complete agreement. Mary and Al both answered "yes, yes" to the loyalty questions, arguing that the willingness to fight for America was the patriotic thing to do. Al was thirty-one and ready to go to war. However, his lungs had been weakened by a bout with pleurisy, which left him unable to serve. Mary was willing to join the Women's Army Corps, but because of her arthritis, she was also unable to serve.

Following the call to enlist, 1,256 Nisei men judged physically fit did volunteer to leave the internment camps and serve in the US Armed Forces. They became part of the 442nd Regimental Combat Team, a segregated company that chose the phrase *Go for Broke* as their fighting slogan. By the end of the war, approximately fourteen thousand Japanese Americans had served in the 442nd, which earned fame as one of the most decorated units in American military history. The valor of these soldiers was so great that a total of 18,143 awards were given to members of this unit, including 9,486 Purple Hearts and 21 Medals of Honor, thirteen of them posthumously.

These soldiers, and Hawaiian Japanese American soldiers from the Hundredth Company, were stationed at Camp Shelby, Mississippi, located a short distance from Jerome. When these homesick Nisei soldiers were on furlough, they turned up by the hundreds at the gates of Jerome Relocation Camp regularly every night, looking for incarcerated relatives or friends from home or just a friendly Japanese face. Mary Tsukamoto and fellow internee Mary Nakahara organized simple Japanese meals and entertainment for these soldiers. On at least one occasion, Mary chaperoned a group of young ladies from Jerome who were permitted to travel to Camp Shelby for a dinner and dance under the auspices of the USO.

Those internees who answered with an unqualified "yes, yes" to Questions 27 and 28 on the loyalty questionnaire were placed on a list of individuals who were cleared for day passes, short-term leaves, long-term leaves in order to enroll at a university, or permanent release if they could find employment outside the West Coast zone of exclusion (Howard 2008, 200). Mary's sister, Ruth, and her husband, Hugh Kiino, were released from Jerome when they were offered jobs in Kalamazoo in southwest Michigan. Within a short time they were able to secure a job for Al, too, so he was cleared for release as well. Once he was settled in Kalamazoo, the young husband sent for his wife and daughter, who were permitted to leave Jerome on November 17, 1943. Together, the family celebrated Al and Mary's seventh wedding anniversary. In the spring of 1944, Mary's parents, her sister Julia, and her brother George were also released to travel to Kalamazoo. By then George had graduated from Jerome's Denson High School. In August 1944, George was drafted into the 442nd and deployed to England.

Although the Tsukamoto family still owned their farm in Florin and more than ever wanted to return there, the government ban on individuals of Japanese ancestry living on the West Coast was still in force. A court case ended the ban. Mitsuye Endo, a resident of Sacramento employed as a civil servant, had been sent to Tule Lake War Relocation Camp in Northern California. She filed a lawsuit charging that her incarceration was unconstitutional, and on December 18, 1944, the Supreme Court ruled in her favor, declaring that the federal government had no legal authority to detain any American citizen without due process and without just cause (Grapes 2001, 26–27). The next day, President Roosevelt lifted the ban. Finally, Mary and her family could return to Florin.

When the Tsukamotos returned to Florin on July 10, 1945, they found their home intact and their farm had been well cared for in their absence by their friend and neighbor, Mr. Bob Fletcher. The Tsukamotos had been gone exactly three years and forty-two days. The next month, the United States dropped atomic bombs on the Japanese cities of Nagasaki and Hiroshima, and the Empire of Japan surrendered to the United States. World War II was finally over. The Tsukamotos greeted this news with a mixture of joy, pride, relief, and sorrow. Al's parents had emigrated from Hiroshima. Following the bombing, they learned that none of their family members still left in Japan had survived, and their home city was leveled to the ground. Mary's in-laws greeted this news with stoicism. "War is a terrible thing," Kuzo and Ito reflected (Tsukamoto and Pinkerton 1988, 207).

Not every internee enjoyed a happy homecoming, and not every internee adjusted well to life after release from camp. Mary's sister, Julia Dakuzaku, was sensitive, artistic, and prone to depression; she struggled against the intense shame and guilt of her internment and had difficulty coping with the prejudice she encountered in Kalamazoo. To ease her pain, Julia decided to serve her country by enlisting in the Women's Army Corps (WAC). She was stationed in Pasco, Washington. Far from home, family, and friends, Julia's emotional pain was not eased. Six weeks after their return to Florin, Mary's parents received a government telegram informing them that Julia had committed suicide on September 9, 1945, exactly one month after the bombing of Nagasaki. Her flag-draped coffin arrived the next day. The suicide became a closely guarded family secret; some of Mary's relatives didn't learn the whole truth about Julia's death until years later (Howard 2008, 230).

The first harvest season after the Tsukamotos returned to Florin, the former internees helped their neighbor Bob Fletcher with the grape harvest. Although the vines were on Tsukamoto land, that harvest belonged to Bob. The next season, Al resumed farming on his own land, and Mary quickly became involved in community activities, including volunteer work for the Women's Society of Christian Service, serving on the faculty of the Tahoe Youth Institute, teaching Sunday school classes, leading a Girl Scouts troop, and working for the PTA. Marielle was enrolled as a student at Florin Grammar School and attended classes in the very same room where Mary had been a student twenty years before.

By 1949, Al and Mary came to the conclusion, reluctantly, that their farm could no longer financially sustain their family of six. Al decided to pull out their grapevines and quit farming, and the couple began to consider available job opportunities. Al accepted a position repairing electronic communications equipment at the newly opened Sacramento Signal Depot. Mary looked to the school for employment and was persuaded by Isabelle Jackson, the principal of her daughter's school, to consider becoming a teacher.

After an absence of thirteen years from college, Mary decided to return to school to complete the courses required to earn her teaching credential. She enrolled at Sacramento State College, simultaneously working as a substitute teacher to gain valuable classroom experience. Later that year, on an emergency credential, Mary accepted a position as a third grade teacher at Florin Elementary School in the Elk Grove School District. Mary became one of the first certificated Japanese American teachers in the United States. She worked as a teacher in the Elk Grove District for twenty-six years, retiring in 1976. In her honor, a new school named Mary Tsukamoto Elementary School was opened in Elk Grove in 1992.

Throughout her teaching career and continuing into her retirement, Mary worked tirelessly for educational projects. In 1959, Mary was selected legislative chairperson on the State Board of the California Council on Education. She was an active member of the Association for Childhood Education International (ACEI). She also worked through her church on Methodist Overseas Relief Work, devoting her energy to the Heifer Project and local projects organized by the Peace Center in Sacramento.

In April 1977, Mary was invited to serve on a community board that created a nonprofit, private summer school for Japanese American children that was devoted to the exploration and promotion of Japanese cultural heritage. The school, named Jan Ken Po Gakko, offered a curriculum that included games, folklore, music, field trips, language, and interaction between the generations. This program was, in many ways, similar to the Japanese language schools that had been established prior to World War II. Mary continued her work for Jan Ken Po for five years.

200

Mary's most important mission, however, was working for Japanese American civil liberties, multicultural understanding, and racial tolerance. On July 21, 1986, Mary received an award as the National JACL Member of the Biennium. That same year, Al and Mary celebrated their golden wedding anniversary. In 1987, during the bicentennial celebration of the Constitution, Mary made a significant contribution to an exhibit about America's Japanese internment camps for the Smithsonian Institution in Washington, DC. She also developed an educational program for Sacramento's California History Museum, entitled *Time of Remembrance*, which educates school children about learning from mistakes made in the past. She donated her letters, journals, and papers to California State University, Sacramento, to inaugurate their Japanese American collection.

In addition, Mary played an important role in the grassroots effort that led to redress for Japanese American citizens who had been incarcerated during the war. In August 1981, she testified during the Congressional hearings held by the United States Commission on Wartime Internment and Relocation of Civilians. Her testimony helped win the passage of the Civil Liberties Act of 1988, signed into law by President Ronald Reagan. Through this legislation, the federal government formally apologized for the internment of the Japanese American community and granted each surviving detainee a restitution payment of twenty thousand dollars.

Mary Tsukamoto passed away of natural causes January 6, 1998, at the age of eighty-two. For her many lifetime achievements, she was named by the California State Senate as a Notable Californian, and she was recognized in March 2006 as one of only ten women who were honored that year by the National Women's History Project.

Teacher Sandra Adickes socializes with a group of Freedom School students in Hattiesburg, Mississippi, during Freedom Summer. 1964. Reprinted with permission from McCain Library and Archives, University of Southern Mississippi.

11

SANDRA ADICKES
She Taught in a Civil Rights Freedom School

To refuse to face the task of creating a vision of a future America
immeasurably more just and noble and beautiful than the America
of today is to evade the most crucial, difficult,
and important educational task.
GEORGE S. COUNTS

On the Fourth of July 1964, in the middle of a hot, sweltering summer afternoon, Sandra Adickes, a young English teacher from New York City, stepped cautiously off a Greyhound bus and into the shabby bus terminal of Hattiesburg, Forrest County, Mississippi. She made a quick telephone call to report the safe arrival of her group and, within minutes, was greeted warmly by Reverend Bob Beech, a volunteer from the Delta Ministry Project. After the tired, hungry, and sweaty group piled themselves and their belongings into the clergyman's car, he drove them to Vernon Dahmer's farm in the nearby black community of Palmer's Crossing, five miles north of downtown Hattiesburg. Vernon had organized a Fourth of July picnic and fish fry to celebrate the nation's day of freedom. This party also served to welcome the visitors and kick-off Hattiesburg's Freedom Summer project.

Sandra and her fellow travelers had boarded the bus in Memphis, Tennessee, just before 7:00 a.m. that morning, and as the bus rolled through miles and miles of oppressively humid southern countryside, Sandra was surprised by the noticeable lack of patriotic display. What she did notice, however, was a billboard on the highway—a political endorsement for a mental health bill by President John F. Kennedy. Someone had flung a can of paint at the oversized sign, splattering the handsome image of the young president who had been slain in Dallas, Texas, just eighteen months previously. When the fatigued and famished group finally arrived at Vernon Dahmer's farm, recalled Sandra, the Fourth of July festivities were "… the first sign I had seen that day of an event honoring our nation's independence," (Adickes 2005, 55).

The guests who attended Vernon's exuberant celebration were civil rights activists, summer volunteers from out-of-state like Sandra, and members of the local black community, young and old, who were also involved in the civil rights movement. The revelers parked themselves under leafy trees, on wooden picnic benches pushed into the shade, or on the dropped-down tailgates of old, rusty trucks. They ate a sumptuous feast that included a typical Southern dish—catfish that had been deep fried in large, dome-bottomed cast iron pots and was served piping hot on paper plates. They toured the cotton fields of Vernon's two-hundred-acre farm on a tractor-drawn flatbed and examined dry, brittle branches sprouting cotton bolls, which had burst open, revealing the downy white cotton within. Near sundown, they gathered together to stand cross-armed in unity and sang freedom songs.

204

As twilight approached, the festivities wound down, for it was essential to everyone's safety to be indoors by nightfall. The local white community, some of whom openly flaunted their membership in the Ku Klux Klan, viewed the arrival of the Freedom Summer volunteers as an unwelcome invasion, and the mixed-race gathering at Vernon's farm was anathema to them. An outbreak of violence was a distinct possibility. Sandra was quickly introduced to Mrs. Addie Mae Jackson, an African American participant in the movement, who would be her hostess for the summer, and the two new allies departed for the Jackson home. As Sandra fell into bed that night, joyful but exhausted, she contemplated the circumstances that had brought her to Mississippi that summer.

Sandra Elaine Adickes was born during the throes of the Great Depression in New York City, July 14, 1933. Like most Americans, Sandra's parents, August and Edythe Oberschlake Adickes, and her sister, Joanne, were not immune to the economic stress so prevalent during that time. In fact, Sandra remembers a period when her father was separated from the family for a year because he went south to work for the Civilian Conservation Corps. "... He never wanted to speak of it," Sandra recalled, "out of the shame of being out of work that afflicted so many men in that time" (Adickes 2005, 32). As the country slowly and painstakingly pulled itself out of the Depression, the Adickes family's fortunes also improved, and by the time Sandra was a teenager, they were comfortably established in a thriving suburb in New Jersey.

After graduating from high school, Sandra attended Douglass College, the women's college associated with Rutgers University. She earned her bachelor's degree in English in 1954 from Douglass, her master's in English education from Hunter College in 1964, and her PhD from New York University in 1977.

Sandra accepted her first position as an English teacher in a vocational high school for girls in the Yorkville section of Manhattan. The school was situated among high-rise luxury apartments occupied by upper-income residents, but the building, which Sandra described as "a treeless, lawnless fortress," and her students, mostly African American and Puerto Rican adolescents from welfare families, did not reflect the affluence of the neighborhood. The facility provided occupational training in marketable job skills, such as secretarial studies, nursing, cosmetology, and needle trades. Sandra's employment in this school was short-lived, however; soon after the conclusion of her first year, school authorities decided the program was obsolete and closed the facility (Adickes 2005, 23-24).

The following year, Sandra was hired to teach English at Benjamin Franklin High School in East Harlem, located along the serenely flowing East River on a tree-lined street between East 114th and East 116th Streets. Franklin High, first opened in 1934 by Leonard Covello, was visually impressive, featuring the grandeur of scale and dramatic use of columns that characterizes a neoclassical structure. Over the portico sheltering the school's entrance, a triangular pediment highlighted a bas relief bust of Benjamin Franklin, an American patriot and a founding father of the American Enlightenment.

The scholastic reputation of Franklin High, however, was not so impressive. In its early years, the school offered creative, innovative, and interactive educational programs, actively encouraging and enjoying a high level of parental and community involvement. Over twenty years later, however, the facility was considered New York City's lowest-performing academic high school. Sandra soon discovered, to her great disappointment, that expectations were low for both teachers and students. Despite an atmosphere of apathy and cynicism, the idealistic, conscientious, and energetic Sandra sought to surround herself with a cohort of young colleagues who worked together to share best practices, generate meaningful classroom experiences, and create a positive influence on the lives of their students. Sandra felt her four years at Franklin High were a mixture of hits and misses, but it would be the summer at the end of her third year when she would truly find her noble purpose.

That year was the summer of 1963. Sandra was thirty years old. Tall, slender, and long-limbed, she wore her shoulder-length blonde hair parted on the left, swept to the right, and held in place by a simple barrette. Everything about Sandra's appearance was simple. The young teacher had a penchant for wearing sleeveless dresses in light fabrics, cinched at the waist, flared at the hip, with a hemline just below the knees; she worked barelegged in flats and wore no makeup.

Sandra had agreed to devote her summer vacation to teaching African American students in Prince Edward County, Virginia, a sleepy little Southern hamlet situated in flatlands streaked by creeks that feed into larger rivers or tranquil lakes. Appomattox, the historic site where General Robert E. Lee surrendered to Northern troops to end the War Between the States, was just over the county line. Annual Civil War reenactments are still a favorite pastime for the locals. In the 1960s, only about fourteen thousand people lived in the area, but the people were plucky. Prince Edward is the only place in the country where the students themselves initiated a court case that went all the way to the United States Supreme Court.

The case involved equality in educational opportunity. The feisty black students of Prince Edward were enrolled in a school that was drastically inferior to the schools provided for white students. Their facility was insufferably overcrowded and shamefully equipped. Some of the buildings were nothing more than plywood shanties, and when administrators ran out of classroom space, they turned an immobile school bus parked on the property into a supplementary classroom. The school provided no desks, no blackboards, no gymnasium, no cafeteria, and no teacher restrooms. When the students formally asked the local school board to allocate money to refurbish their facility, the request was flatly denied. Black students, they declared, didn't deserve such luxuries. In protest, the students walked out and filed a lawsuit. The case was tied up in the courts for years, finally becoming incorporated into the landmark case *Brown vs. Board of Education*, in which the US Supreme Court formally ordered an end to segregation in the nation's public schools. Prince Edward County authorities closed down all the schools in their district rather than integrate. The schools stayed closed for five long years.

During that five-year period, a series of private schools funded by state money and tax credits from the county were opened to educate white students. These schools were collectively known as Prince Edward Academy or "segregation academies." The black students received no instruction, unless they moved in with relatives in a neighboring county or set up their own makeshift classrooms. Most African American students got no education at all, and by 1963, only about five percent of the county's black children were enrolled in any school. In an attempt to fill some of the void that five years of instructional neglect had created, Queens College in New York City recruited volunteer educators to come to Prince Edward County during the summer of 1963 to participate in a remedial program they entitled "Operation Catch-Up." Sandra Adickes was one of the thirty teachers, sixteen college students, and one university professor who answered the call. At summer's end, some of the volunteers continued their work into the next academic year, and when the schools in Prince Edward County were finally reopened in the fall of 1964, the classrooms were integrated at last.

The following year, in the summer of 1964, the Student Nonviolent Coordinating Committee (SNCC), inspired by the Virginia project, organized a similar project for Mississippi as part of their ambitious Freedom Summer agenda. Mississippi, too, had long neglected the education of its African American youths. It was the only state in the Union that did not have a compulsory education law on the books. Graduation rates in general were abysmal; only 47 percent of the white students finished high school, while only 7 percent of the blacks did. In Mississippi, the state spent four times more money per learner on the white students than on the black students. The SNCC sought to bridge at least some of that gap (Watson 2010, 137–138).

Although providing educational opportunities was a major goal of the Mississippi project, SNCC's primary objective was to increase African American participation in the voting process. The organization believed the best way to achieve lasting positive change was to increase the involvement of black citizens in the democratic process. They targeted Mississippi because that state had the lowest percentage of African American voter participation in the country. In 1962, only 6.7 percent of black citizens eligible to vote were registered. This low turnout was the result of many deliberate discriminatory tactics that were used by whites to systematically block their attempts to register. Among these tactics were exclusionary maneuvers, intimidation, threats, poll taxes, poll tests, or outright violence.

During her service in the Prince Edward project, Sandra Adickes and fellow-activist Norma Becker, a junior high school social studies teacher also from New York, were recruited to participate in the Mississippi summer project by Ivanhoe Donaldson, a staff member of the SNCC. Typically, volunteers were required to be at least eighteen years of age, be able to pay their own expenses, be willing to live with African American families, and, most importantly, be courageous enough to face danger in an intensely hostile political environment. Most of the volunteers were white college students from northern and western states who came from affluent families. The parents of these students could well afford to supply sufficient funds to cover living expenses for the summer, five hundred dollars in emergency bail money, and transportation home if the situation became too volatile (Boyd 2004, 171). As an employed teacher with an annual salary of $7,200, Sandra was able to pay her own way.

Prior to heading to Mississippi, Freedom Summer volunteers were required to attend a week-long orientation meeting. Many of the volunteers, both male and female, attended their training session at the Western College for Women in Oxford, Ohio, but because her teaching assignment in New York City had not yet ended when the Ohio sessions were conducted, Sandra attended hers at LeMoune College in Memphis, Tennessee. At this orientation meeting, the idealistic recruits were warned about the hazardous conditions they would likely face in the Jim Crow South, were tutored in the philosophy of nonviolent resistance, and were drilled in strategies for self-protection. "We had to tell these young people exactly what they were getting ready to get involved in," recalled SNCC staff member Hollis Watkins. "They had to be prepared to go to jail, they had to be prepared to be beaten, and they had to be prepared to be killed. And if they were not prepared for either one or all three of those, then they probably should reconsider coming to Mississippi" (Boyd 2004, 171).

These were not empty threats. On June 21, 1964, the very first day of Mississippi's Freedom Summer, three men who had been present at the Ohio orientation—two SNCC staff members, Michael Schwerner and James Chaney, and volunteer Andrew Goodman—disappeared while investigating the firebombing of the church facility designated for their voter recruitment activities. At the end of the summer, on August 4, their badly beaten and bullet-ridden bodies were discovered buried in an earthen dam in Neshoba County. During the ten weeks of Mississippi's Freedom Summer, a total of four civil rights activists lost their lives, three African Americans involved in the movement were murdered, four were critically wounded, eighty Freedom Summer workers were beaten, and 1,062 were arrested. In addition, thirty-seven churches were firebombed, and thirty African American homes or businesses were torched.

Nearly two weeks after the disappearance of Schwerner, Chaney, and Goodman, on Independence Day, Sandra completed her orientation and arrived at the Mississippi Freedom School established at the Priest Creek Missionary Baptist Church. The church was located in Palmer's Crossing, a dusty little suburb of Hattiesburg that featured no paved streets, no traffic lights, no signs, and where nearly every store in town was a "salvage store." In those days, the main town of Hattiesburg, which Sandra once commented fit the cliché "sleepy southern town" (Adickes 2005,

1), was home to about 35,000 residents. It was situated in southern Mississippi about a hundred miles north of the Gulf Coast, in the midst of a longleaf pine forest at the fork of the Bouie and Leaf Rivers. The Priest Creek School where Sandra was assigned was one of seven Freedom Schools, a community center, and three libraries that were established in and around the Hattiesburg area that summer.

In the months leading up to the project, Sandra and Norma Becker worked tirelessly to prepare for Freedom Summer. Together they recruited forty teachers from the New York City area to join the project. They petitioned sponsorship from their local teachers' union, raised funds to support the project, solicited contributions of books for the libraries, and collected supplies and suitable teaching materials for the classrooms. Additionally, they worked on a committee to create a curriculum that addressed their students' basic literacy needs in various subjects such as reading, writing, mathematics, and verbal skills. Lesson plans emphasized citizenship and knowledge of the Constitution, African American history, leadership development, and current events, including the most recent developments in the civil rights movement. The curriculum also included electives, such as typing, French, Spanish, German, literature, creative writing, art, drama, story-telling, and dance. Instructional strategies placed emphasis on student participation, the Socratic method, and incorporating the abundant use of the "call-and-response" method so familiar to the African American community.

Preparations complete, Sandra and the other volunteer teachers assigned to the seven Hattiesburg Freedom Schools expected a total of about 150 students to show up for registration. They were taken by surprise when 575 appeared. The first student to register was an eighty-two-year-old man who had taught himself to read, but who needed help with the registration form. All seven schools boasted overflowing enrollment (Watson 2010, 139).

Despite the formality of the coursework, classes were conducted in a relaxed and casual manner and were often held outside. Students sheltered under the low, leafy branches of a sweet gum, chinaberry, or live oak tree; sprawled on the cool grass; sat on the shady porch steps of a church; or found somewhere else that offered some comfort from the sweltering Mississippi heat. Students called their teachers by their first names, and Sandra appreciated the informality.

Freedom School teachers quickly learned that black Mississippi school children had long been trained to "stay in their place," and independent thought and initiative were actively discouraged. After some initial reticence, though, the young participants soon relaxed and responded positively to Sandra's dynamic question-and-answer teaching strategy. "This method liberated students from the stifling memorization of stale curriculum in their segregated schools," recalled Sandra. "It was the approach I had developed in my teaching, but my Freedom School students responded more enthusiastically than any other group I had ever taught because they had never been permitted, let alone encouraged to voice their own answers to questions and ask their own questions" (Adickes 2005, 58).

Hattiesburg's black students had long become accustomed to receiving battered, out-of-date and obsolete textbooks, which had been discarded by the white schools. Mississippi's African American teachers had never been allowed to teach black history or the contributions of blacks to American society or to explore literature written by black authors. So Sandra was especially elated when she placed into each student's eager hands newly printed copies of *Black Boy* by Mississippi native son Richard Wright and *Go Tell It on the Mountain* by James Baldwin.

The Palmer's Creek teachers quickly established a routine. In the mornings, the 8:00 a.m. session opened with a presentation, followed by small group discussion, and then instruction on individual subject areas, which lasted until 11:00. Next came a lunch break, followed by meetings or community activities, and then another school session for the adults met in the evenings between 7:30 and 9:30 p.m. Volunteers were also expected to assist with the voter registration drives. On top of those responsibilities, there were also a couple of occasions when, hearing about a threat to firebomb the school, Sandy courageously spent a tension-filled night on guard duty. The schedule was grueling, to say the least.

On the last day of summer school, Friday, August 14, 1964, some of Sandra's students were eager to put into practice the lessons they had learned in her class. The young teacher was concerned about protecting the kids from a violent confrontation, but the young people were persistent, and Sandra finally agreed to what appeared to be the safest undertaking. She accompanied six of them on an excursion to the downtown Hattiesburg Library in a quest to get public library cards. She knew they were determined to go, with or without her, and she figured her presence might keep them from getting arrested. The students were eleven-year-old Curtis Duckworth, and teenagers Gwen Merritt, Carolyn Moncure, Diane Moncure, La Verne Reed, and Jimmella Stokes. Sandra regarded the excursion as "… in effect, a graduation trip."

Together, Sandra and the young people, all identically dressed in blue chambray work shirts that formed part of the SNCC uniform, rode the city bus into town. They entered the library, requested library cards, and asked to use the library facilities. The clerk on duty, a blonde woman in her twenties, was thunderstruck. "Her eyes nearly bolted from their sockets," remembered Sandra, as the clerk nervously summoned her supervisor (Adickes 2005, 90). The students politely repeated their request, but the supervisor adamantly refused, whispering urgently that the kids were challenging a social custom that had been practiced in Hattiesburg since long before they were born. Their actions, she complained, could negatively impact library patrons throughout the entire town. Two weeks previously, authorities had already decided to shut down the library rather than integrate. The supervisor ordered Sandra and her students to leave immediately, but the determined students insisted on completing their mission. Finally, the frustrated supervisor called the police. Twenty minutes later, Chief of Police Hugh Herring arrived. He promptly closed the library for an "unscheduled inventory" and ejected Sandra and her students from the building.

Following their expulsion from the library, Sandra and her students decided to get something to eat, so they made their way to the lunch counter at the local Kress store. They seated themselves in two booths near the lunch counter and asked to be served. In compliance with the newly enacted Civil Rights Act of 1964, the waitress allowed the students to place their orders, but obeying a directive from the store manager, she refused to serve Sandra. "We have to serve the colored," the flustered waitress blurted out, "but we are not going to serve the whites that come in with them" (Adickes 2005, 91).

The students decided to leave rather than to eat without their teacher. When they emerged from the store, Sandra, who had been under surveillance by the Hattiesburg police from the time that she and the students left the library, was confronted by local police officers. Sandra was arrested for vagrancy and taken to jail where she was photographed, fingerprinted, and placed in a cell. The local office of the Council of Federated Organizations (COFO) were informed of Sandra's arrest, and within an hour, COFO lawyers arrived at the jail to post her bail.

The Hattiesburg Library was reopened three days later, on Monday, August 17, 1964. That day, a second attempt to integrate the library was made, this time by teachers and students from the Freedom School established at True Light Baptist Church. Volunteer teachers Ben Achtenberg, Tom Edwards, Bill Jones, and Susan Patterson, and the six students they accompanied, entered the library, asked for cards, and requested library services. Like Sandra, the activists were removed, and the four adults were arrested and jailed for vagrancy. After this incident, true to their promise, authorities closed the Hattiesburg Library indefinitely.

Following the incident at the lunch counter, Sandra filed a lawsuit against the Kress Company for violation of her civil rights. Attorney Eleanor Jackson Piel took on the case, which was sent to federal court but later dismissed. Not accepting defeat, Sandra filed a civil lawsuit. Her case went all the way to the US Supreme Court, and six years later, in 1970, *Adickes vs. Kress & Company* was settled out of court. Sandra generously donated the money she received from the settlement to the Southern Conference Educational Fund to be used for scholarships. Among those who received financial assistance from Sandra's donation was Jimmella Stokes, one of the teenaged activists Sandra had accompanied to the Hattiesburg Library.

The courage, expertise, and dedication of teachers like Sandra Adickes, who were involved in the civil rights movement, actively demonstrated the Founding Fathers' precept that government should derive its power from the people, and it also furthered the American ideal of equal opportunity for all American citizens. By the end of Freedom Summer, more than 3,500 students of all ages from kindergarten to the elderly had attended a Mississippi Freedom School. More than seventeen thousand eligible voters were newly registered throughout the state. Eventually, the tenacious efforts of civil rights activists resulted in the repeal of offensive Jim Crow laws and the full enforcement of the constitutional rights of America's African American citizens. "The knowledge that I was part of a struggle that has made life permanently better for great numbers of people has brought me enduring pride and satisfaction," wrote Sandra in her autobiographical book *Legacy of a Freedom School*. "I also believe, as for years I have been saying to students, that the best thing one can do when one is young is to become involved with a movement dedicated to making life better for others" (Adickes 2005, 5).

At the conclusion of her Mississippi Freedom School experience, Sandra returned to New York City and her teaching post at Benjamin Franklin High School. In the years that followed, Sandra was among a number of Freedom School activists who participated in anti-Vietnam War protests. In New York City, Sandra and Norma Becker organized the *Teachers Committee for Peace in Vietnam*. The accomplishments of this organization included the preparation and distribution of antiwar literature, nonviolent demonstrations for peace, the collection of 2,700 signatures on an antiwar petition, and a full page ad in the *New York Times* urging President Lyndon B. Johnson to bring a swift end to the conflict in Vietnam. The advertisement, published May 30, 1965, was addressed "To Our President, A Former Teacher," a reference to the chief executive's tenure as a junior high schoolteacher in Cotulla, Texas, in 1927, and a high school teacher in Houston, Texas, in 1930 (Adickes 2005, 137).

For several years, Sandra expanded her teaching experiences by working in a variety of public school settings throughout New York City. In September 1965, she accepted a one-year teaching assignment at Erasmus Hall High School, located at 890 Flatbush Avenue in Flatbush, Brooklyn. Erasmus, established by Dutch settlers in 1786 as a private academy, holds the distinction of being the oldest public high school in the country. The school's wooden, clapboard-sided structure was built in the Federal style in 1787. The building was named to the National Registry of Historic Places in 1975. Notable alumni include Founding Fathers Alexander Hamilton and Aaron Burr, Hollywood celebrities Susan Hayward and Mae West, singers Barbra Streisand and Neil Diamond, authors Bernard Malamud and Mickey Spillane, and athletes Waite Hoyt, Sid Luckman, and Cheryl Toussaint.

Sandra's next teaching assignment was a one-year stint at Livingston School, located in Greenwich Village in Lower Manhattan. Livingston was a facility offering programs for emotionally disturbed adolescent girls. Establishing and nurturing positive relationships with students was given the greatest emphasis at this school, and to that end, class sizes were very small, only six to ten students per course. The curriculum included basic literacy skills and vocational education classes in typing, cosmetology, and cooking.

Following her year at Livingston, Sandra accepted her next teaching position at Washington Irving High School, which was located at 40 Irving Place between East Sixteenth and Seventeenth Streets in the borough of Manhattan. Built in 1938 and standing eleven-stories high, the facility is named after American author Washington Irving. At that time, the school was an all-girls' academic high school well-known for its rigorous academic programs, and Sandra appreciated working with colleagues she found to be enlightened and talented (Adickes 2005, 142). Sandra spent three years in this teaching assignment.

In January 1970, Sandra was hired to teach at New York City Technical College, and in 1973, she became an assistant professor of English at the College of Staten Island. In the years that followed, she taught at other campus locations of the City University of New York. When she retired, she became a Professor Emerita in the English Department of Winona State University in Winona, Minnesota.

Sandra Adickes never married, but in 1973, at the age of forty, she adopted a six-year-old African American child, Delores, and in 1996, at the age of sixty-three, she adopted two Chinese-born teenagers, Cynthia and Lily, from Changshu, Jiangsu Province, China. In July, 2012, she celebrated her seventy-ninth birthday.

Advanced Placement Calculus teacher Jaime Escalante, a champion for Latino rights, wears his trademark Escalante hat. 1988. Photo by George Rose/Contributor/Getty Images.

12

Jaime Escalante
He Championed Latino American Students

*The best teachers give their pupils both a sense of
order, discipline, control; and a powerful stimulus
which urges them to take their destinies in their own
hands, kick over rules, and transgress all boundaries.*
Gilbert Highet

The newly hired teacher, driving a beat-up, ten-year-old, pale
green Volkswagen, pulled into the potholed parking lot of James
A. Garfield High School in East Los Angeles. Garfield High, a
neglected campus dating back to 1925, was situated in the middle
of a barrio neighborhood thick with jacaranda trees that dropped
their diminutive lavender blossoms onto run-down stucco houses
fronted by poorly maintained lawns. The decaying campus was
surrounded by chain-link fencing, littered with trash, and marred
by gang graffiti. Nevertheless, with determined and purposeful
strides, the middle-aged teacher crossed the campus grounds and
entered the administration office. It was his first day as an instructor in an American school. This was going to be a challenge, he

knew, but forty-three-year-old Jaime Escalante was confident. He had already overcome so many challenges in his life.

Jaime Alfonso Escalante Gutierrez was born on December 31, 1930, in La Paz, Bolivia. His parents, Zenobio and Sara Escalante, lived and worked in Achacachi, a remote Aymara and Quechua Indian village situated on the Bolivian altiplano, a vast and dry plateau at high altitude, located near the eastern shore of Lake Titicaca in the midst of the Andes Mountains. Both parents were poorly paid government schoolteachers, and the area where they lived and worked was not of their choosing; this was an involuntary teaching assignment. Usually in Bolivia, government schoolteachers battled to survive financially in communities that were economically depressed, and the experience of Zenobio and Sara was typical. Three furnished rooms rented from a La Paz doctor served as the Escalante family's modest living quarters, and this was the most they could afford.

In Achacachi, medical facilities were woefully inadequate, and near the end of her pregnancy, Sara left the village for a temporary stay with relatives in La Paz, four hours away, in order to give birth to her child in the city's more modern hospital facilities. Jaime arrived on the last day of the year, the second of five children. The other children were older sister Olimpia, younger sister Bertha, and two younger brothers, Jose and Raul.

For the poverty-stricken Quechua and Aymara residents of Achacachi, life was a continuous struggle, a hard-fought and primitive agrarian subsistence. The Quechuas are descendants of Indians from the ancient Inca civilization; the Aymaras are an indigenous ethnic group that predates the Incas. As a youngster, Jaime learned to speak the dialects of both, in addition to the dominant culture's Spanish. To entertain himself, he spent his days inventing games, practicing sports, or meandering through Achacachi's central plaza with his beloved maternal grandfather, also a retired teacher, who loved to tease him and test his intellectual abilities with riddles and word puzzles.

Jaime adored his gentle, hardworking, and devoted mother, but his relationship with his father was a different story. Zenobio drank excessively, and when he was under the influence, he was verbally and physically abusive to anyone who had the misfortune to be within reach. Jaime and his siblings spent their after-school hours anywhere but home in order to escape Zenobio's drunken tirades. One day, after years of maltreatment, Sara abruptly packed up her belongings and her children and left Achacachi to move back with her family in La Paz. The single mother and her kids settled into a modest tin-roofed adobe hovel on Graneros Street. Jaime was only nine years old at the time.

Jaime and his siblings welcomed the calmer atmosphere that now permeated their home, but this new environment required some adjustment. On his first day of elementary school in the city, Jaime wore an outfit typical for Aymara children: long pants, a long-sleeved shirt, sandals, and an Indian jacket. At first, the other boys stared incredulously at him, and then they laughed. Jaime soon impressed them, though, with his exceptional skill in arithmetic and his superior athletic abilities; he was especially good at soccer, basketball, and handball (Mathews 1988, 22). At his new school, the most difficult adjustment Jaime had to make was to the formality of the classroom: sitting still, paying attention to the teacher, raising his hand before speaking. He had never been required to adhere to so many school rules before, and it was frustrating for him to bend to so much discipline. Nevertheless, Jaime eventually became accustomed to his new life and would have been reasonably satisfied, if it were not for the intermittent visitations by his father, which were disturbing to everyone in the household. Just like when he lived in Achacachi, Jaime went to great lengths to avoid his father during these visits.

Within a few years, Sara was able to afford a little house on the rugged western slope of the steep hills that surrounded La Paz, in the district known as Sopocachi, one of the longest-standing residential neighborhoods in the city. Their new home, although an improvement from their former dwelling, was still not much more than a drab adobe shack. It was situated on a steep, dusty, dirt road and surrounded by grass and shrubs that only just barely supported the grazing of a few sheep and cows owned by neighbors.

In 1945, when Jaime was fourteen years of age, Sara was able to scrounge up enough money to pay for his tuition to San Calixto High School, one of the most prestigious private schools in La Paz. The institution was founded in 1882, when Andres Santa Cruz, the third president of Bolivia, gifted the property to Catholic Jesuits. San Calixto's picturesque sixteenth-century structure of Spanish Colonial architecture was situated on a narrow cobblestone street named Calle Jenaro Sanjinez, near Bolivia's presidential palace. Inside the school's tall, flat walls of plastered adobe, Jaime found a tranquil environment of sun-drenched, well-tended courtyards, refreshing water fountains, and miniature peach trees. Inside, the walls were covered with ornamental plaques celebrating the academic and athletic achievements of San Calixto's alumni (Schraff 2009, 21–23).

Although Jaime came from the poor side of town, he quickly made a place for himself among the all-male student body, which consisted of 750 mostly upper-class students. And although

224

Jaime frequently earned disapproval from his Jesuit teachers for talking excessively and playing the class clown, he excelled beyond expectations in his courses in physics, mathematics, and engineering. Jaime began to plan a future for himself as an engineer, and he selected an engineering college in Argentina where he intended to enroll after graduation. His plan was derailed, however, on the day his father suddenly collapsed and died, leaving Sara unable to pay for Jaime's post-graduate education. At his father's funeral, Jaime discovered a painful secret about his father: he had another family and had fathered other children—two sons and a daughter. On that day, Jaime was surprised, but not ashamed, when he realized that he was not sorry his father was dead (Mathews 1988, 30–31).

After his graduation from San Calixto High School, Jaime spent an aimless year earning pocket money by doing odd jobs. He spent much of his day lounging at the local watering hole, socializing with friends who also had no jobs and no prospects. The next year, when he was nineteen years old, a series of strikes and minor insurrections broke out in the southern Bolivian valley towns of Sucre and Potosi. In response, acting President Mamerto Urriolagoitia ordered a mobilization of federal armed forces. Jaime and some of his buddies, sensing an opportunity for adventure, decided to enlist. Jaime's stint in the Bolivian army was brief and relatively uneventful, although he did see some action. The short-lived and poorly organized rebellion was quickly repressed, and it was not long before Jaime and his cohorts were honorably discharged.

Once again, Jaime found himself without employment or prospects. Jaime returned to his habit of spending his days socializing with his unemployed buddies. One day, Jaime ran into a high school friend named Roberto Cordero, who was on his way to take the entrance exams at the Escuela Normal Superior Simon Bolivar, one of Bolivia's most prominent teachers' colleges. Roberto attempted to convince Jaime of the advantages of pursuing a career in education. As the son of teachers, Jaime was well aware of how hard a teacher worked, and how poorly a teacher was paid. But, Roberto argued, any job was better than no job, and the work could be very rewarding. Finally, Jaime was persuaded to accompany Roberto to try his luck on the entrance exams. Both men passed their exams with flying colors, and together they enrolled in courses in mathematics, chemistry, and physics.

After completing only two years of coursework at Normal Superior, Jaime discovered that a position had opened up in the Physics Department at the privately run American Institute. Qualified instructors for physics were few and far between, but Jaime's college instructors had already observed his expertise in the subject, and they encouraged him to apply for the job. Jaime went to the interview, armed with a favorable recommendation from one of his university professors, Umberto Bilbao, who just happened to be in charge of recruiting at the Education Ministry. Jaime sailed through the interview and, although he was only twenty-one, had not completed his university coursework, and had no prior teaching experience, he was offered the position.

The new recruit had earned a reputation for his outstanding abilities in physics and mathematics, but he was not scheduled to take classes in methods of instruction until his third year. Jaime was able to discover what teaching strategies he needed through trial and error and by imitating other teachers that he respected and admired. Within a few months, Jaime was offered a second job, teaching physics at the National Bolivar School, a highly regarded public high school located near the American Institute. Not long after that, he triumphantly accepted a third position, teaching physics at his prestigious alma mater, San Calixto. Jaime was astonished that he was able to garner three teaching positions before graduating from teacher training college, and without possessing a credential. It was not until 1954 that he finally completed his university coursework at Normal Superior and obtained his Bolivian teacher's license.

While still a student at Normal Superior, Jaime's friends introduced him to an extremely attractive young classmate named Fabiola Tapia, who was also studying to become a teacher. She was the eldest daughter of a family of devout evangelical Protestants, an uncommon and occasionally persecuted minority in Bolivia (Mathews 1988, 44). Fabiola's father had earned a degree from Biola, the Bible Institute of Los Angeles, a small private college in California. Like Jaime's parents, Fabiola's father was employed by the Bolivian government as a teacher.

Before long, Jaime began to tutor Fabiola in mathematics. She found his unique style of teaching entertaining and, more importantly, effective, and she quickly concluded that this dynamic man possessed an extraordinary talent as an educator. Jaime and Fabiola began to see each other socially, often going for long walks to the downtown area, where they shared saltenas, Jaime's favorite Bolivian snack. Saltenas are made from thick yellow pastry dough wrapped around beef, eggs, tomatoes, beans, baby peas, onions, and garlic, and held together with paper.

Unlike other women that Jaime had dated, Fabiola was serious, sensible, hardworking, and pious—qualities that Jaime admired. Jaime proposed, and the two were married at the Calama Street Baptist Church in Cochabamba on November 25,

1954. They honeymooned in the altiplano city of Oruro, and then they made their home in a little rented house half a block away from Jaime's mother. The following year, their first child, Jaime, Jr., was born.

To support his family, Jaime settled into a demanding schedule of teaching. In the mornings, he taught at San Calixto. In the afternoons, he taught at National Bolivar; he also conducted late classes at the Commercial High School. In the evenings, he taught at a military academy night school and tutored private students. Despite working four jobs and tutoring on the side, Jaime was still struggling to provide financially for his family. The continuing instability of the political situation in Bolivia created additional stress, and Fabiola began a campaign to persuade Jaime that greater opportunities awaited them all if they immigrated to the United States. Jaime was resistant to the suggestion. He had worked very hard to establish himself in La Paz, and he didn't want to give it all up and start over.

During this time, Jaime threw his energy into organizing a group of his brightest San Calixto students to compete in a challenging citywide competition in chemistry, physics, and mathematics. To prepare for the competition, Jaime's students were subjected to a grueling schedule of intense study and repetitious practice, against which the students sometimes rebelled. But Jaime, driven and stubborn, overpowered their resistance. His efforts paid off when the students emerged victorious, and his reputation as a skillful educator increased.

Jaime's unorthodox and sometimes harsh teaching style occasionally frightened his students, but it also motivated them. He was not afraid to yell at his kids for being tardy or lazy, but he also gave them encouragement and taught them to believe in themselves. "The key, for the teacher as well as for the student, is hard work. Hard work makes the future," Jaime emphasized. "When hard work is combined with love, humor, and a recognition of the *ganas*—the desire to learn, the ability to sacrifice, the wish to get ahead—that burns in our young people, the stereotypes and the barriers begin to crumble," he once explained (Escalante and Dirmann 1990). This point of view became the foundation for Jaime's teaching philosophy throughout his entire career.

In 1961, Jaime was invited to spend a year in San Juan, Puerto Rico, as part of President John F. Kennedy's new *Alliance for Progress*. The program offered specialized training to industrial arts and science teachers from Latin America in order to improve educational programs and fight poverty. As part of this program, Jaime visited the White House, shook the hand of President Kennedy, toured the State Department, attended an international education conference in Pittsburgh, and examined an innovative new physics laboratory in a Tennessee high school. Jaime was impressed, and the experience convinced him to seriously consider Fabiola's suggestion to move to the United States.

It wasn't until 1963, however, that Jaime was finally able to leave Bolivia. Immigration papers in hand, he flew into Los Angeles International Airport on Christmas Eve and was met by his wife's brother, Samuel Tapia, who had agreed to be the Escalantes' official sponsor. Jaime moved in with Samuel and another of Sara's brothers, high-school-aged David, in their yellow wood-framed house on Wilson Avenue in Pasadena, a northeastern suburb of Los Angeles. Pasadena derived its name from a Chippewa Indian word meaning "crown of the valley" and is known internationally for its annual New Year's Day Rose Parade and Rose Bowl festivities. The neighborhood was a good choice, for the locals readily accepted new immigrants, the rent was cheap, and the local college, Pasadena City College (PCC), had a reputation for providing special assistance programs to its foreign-born students (Mathews 1988, 55).

When Jaime arrived in Pasadena, he was thirty-three years old, and he couldn't speak a word of English. Although he had a degree in education, a credential in mathematics, twelve years of teaching experience, and an excellent reputation in his profession in Bolivia, he did not meet the requirements for employment as a teacher in the United States. In order to return to the teaching profession, Jaime would have to start all over—learn a new language, earn a new degree in mathematics from an American university, and acquire a California teaching credential.

Determined to make a success of his new beginning, the new immigrant rolled up his sleeves and went to work. He watched countless hours of television in order to learn English, and he enrolled in classes at PCC. Meanwhile, in order to make ends meet, he took a job as a busboy and dishwasher at the Van de Kamp's Restaurant located across the street from the college. With money he'd brought with him from Bolivia, he bought a new 1964 Volkswagen beetle, pale green in color, the automobile which would later become his signature vehicle. By the time Fabiola and eight-year-old Jaime, Jr., arrived in the United States in May of 1964, Jaime's boss at Van de Kamp had recognized the new immigrant's value, and had promoted him to a position as the restaurant's cook.

The reunited family moved into a small, one-bedroom guesthouse rented from Fabiola's brother, Sam. Jaime's young son, Jaime, Jr., considered his new life in California an adventure, but Fabiola found it harder to adjust. Soon after her arrival she began pressing her husband to find a better-paying job, one with greater status, more commensurate with his level of education and experience.

After some time, Jaime finally felt functional enough in English to apply for a position as an electronics technician for the Burroughs Corporation, a manufacturer of office machines. Jaime's bosses quickly discovered his expertise in electronics, and he was promoted. At one point, the company even offered him a position as the manager for a new plant they were opening in Mexico, but Jaime declined the job offer because he wanted to remain in the United States. All the while, he continued with his courses at Pasadena City College. In 1967, Jaime earned an associate of arts degree with a double major in mathematics and physics. The Escalante family celebrated more joy when, in 1969, Fabiola gave birth to the couple's second son, Fernando (Morey and Dunn, 1996, 20).

It wasn't until 1973 that Jaime finally completed all of the requirements for his bachelor of arts degree from California State University, Los Angeles. Upon his graduation, he also won a scholarship from the National Science Foundation, a federally funded agency whose goal was to promote American progress in mathematics, computer science, and social science. This scholarship enabled him to complete the requirements for his teaching credential by the end of the following year, since it provided money for tuition and books, plus a stipend of $150 per week for living expenses. It had taken him ten long years of hard work, but at last Jaime was prepared to resume his teaching career.

Jaime applied for a teaching position with the Los Angeles Unified School District and was elated when he was hired to instruct classes in computer science at Garfield High. However, on the first day of the school year in September 1974, Jaime seriously doubted the wisdom of his decision. The student population at Garfield was 95 percent Hispanic and 80 percent lived in poverty. The campus was rife with graffiti and trash. The students were unruly, disrespectful, foul-mouthed, and sometimes violent. The school suffered from gang fights, drug problems, unplanned pregnancies, high absenteeism, and high dropout rates (Morey and Dunn, 1996, 20-21). Instead of the promised computer classes, Jaime was given five periods of basic math and a textbook containing material at about the fifth-grade level. He was told that Garfield students were not capable of work at a higher level. Jaime went home at the end of his first day sadly disappointed and greatly discouraged.

Despite Jaime's initial reservations, again he rolled up his shirt sleeves and went to work. He had devoted ten years of his life toward the goal of returning to the classroom, and he was not about to give up without a fight. Jaime decorated his classroom with sports posters and banners featuring inspirational sayings. He used creative strategies to teach complicated math concepts. For example, he would bring a razor-sharp meat cleaver and, dressed in a chef's hat and apron, chop up an apple to teach the class about fractions, circumference, and diameter. This was an instructional strategy he learned from his mother. He would wear silly hats, crack jokes, use props, create sports metaphors, utilize music and posters, and do whatever else he could think of to get his students' attention.

"I learned early in my career that teaching is fun—at least, it should be fun. Students learn better when they are having a good time," Jaime once expounded. "While I teach respect and discipline and I demand a great deal of hard work from my students,

I always try to do it in a way that is fun. I use toys, tell lots of jokes, and let the kids participate. A teacher must enjoy his or her work, and convey that joy to the students," he asserted (Escalante and Dirmann 1990). Everything he did, from his exaggerated facial expressions and his classroom theatrics to his silly nicknames or his sarcastic remarks, was part of a deliberate plan to boost the academic performance of his students. Even the monotony of his wardrobe was calculated to reduce distraction. To the casual observer, it seemed as if he wore the same slacks, shirt, tie, and newsboy cap every day. That cap became his trademark. In fact, the style is so closely associated with Jaime that in Bolivia, it is known as an "Escalante hat" (Byers 1996, 64).

Because of his passion for teaching, Jaime returned to Garfield for a second year. To his surprise, he found that all of the school's administrators had been fired or reassigned. Students at the school had been performing so poorly that WASC, the Western Association of Schools and Colleges, threatened to revoke the school's accreditation if substantial improvement could not be demonstrated. Jaime seized the opportunity to push for some changes he adamantly believed were necessary. He had always argued that teachers must challenge their students with rigorous coursework, rather than dilute the curriculum to the lowest level possible. With a new administration in place, Jaime negotiated for tougher courses. He began by teaching some introductory algebra classes, and it was not long before Garfield's students began to rise to the challenge. Even the students that had been labeled by others as "unteachable" were demonstrating significant progress.

By 1979, Jaime initiated the first calculus class offered at Garfield High, although only five students enrolled in the course. At the end of the year, those five students were expected to take the Advanced Placement (AP) exam, a standardized test that awarded college credits to students who earned a score of 3 or better on a scale of 1 to 5. The test was so difficult that only 2 percent of American high school students even attempted it. Before even enrolling in the calculus course, each student had to master Algebra 2, trigonometry, and mathematical analysis. Jaime was thrilled when four out of the five calculus students passed the Calculus AP exam that year.

Jaime was so encouraged by these results that the next year he worked even harder to recruit more students for his advanced program. To ensure their success on the demanding test, he conducted summer school classes to establish a solid foundation in mathematics, and then during the school year, he required the students to attend daily hour-and-a-half-long after-school sessions and all-day Saturday classes. If the students were struggling, he tutored them before school or during their lunch hour. Most importantly, he persuaded their parents to become involved, convincing them to insist that their children attend school regularly and complete their homework consistently.

Before long, Jaime had gained his students' deep respect and lasting affection. They gave him the nickname Kimo, short for Kimo Sabe, meaning "the man who knows," an allusion to the character in the 1950s television show *The Lone Ranger*. There was no real physical resemblance between the tall, slender, athletic hero of the TV program and the short, stout educator with the square-rimmed glasses and thinning hair from Bolivia. "His thick brown fingers swept the air when he lectured and ground chalk into the blackboard with an audible crack," described Jaime's biographer, Jay Mathews. "He had a stocky build, a large square head with a prominent jaw, and a widening bald spot covered with a few stray

234

hairs, like a threadbare victory wreath on a Bolivian Caesar. He looked oddly like the school mascot, a gruff bulldog, and exuded a sense of mischief ..." (Mathews 1988, 3). Clearly, though, the students recognized Jaime as an outstanding role model and a man with knowledge.

By 1982, eighteen students were enrolled in Jaime's AP Calculus class, the highest number of any AP class he had taught thus far. Like the preceding three years, the teacher and his students studied and practiced relentlessly to master the challenging coursework. Unfortunately, just at a crucial point in their preparation for the AP exam, in March of 1982, Jaime suffered a mild heart attack. He hadn't felt well all day, and during that evening's night course, Jaime passed out and fell down a flight of stairs, landing unconscious on the linoleum floor at the bottom. Although he sustained a deep cut over one eye, he went back to his classroom and attempted to finish the lesson. Finally admitting that he was too incapacitated to continue, he dismissed the class and, astonishingly, was able to drive himself home. When he went inside, Jaime, Jr., took one look at his father and insisted on taking him to the hospital immediately. In the emergency room, the gash over Jaime's eye was stitched, and the protesting and headstrong patient was admitted for observation. Jaime was an annoying and recalcitrant patient, and finally his doctor sent him home with orders that he rest for at least two weeks. Fabiola drove him home from the hospital, and Jaime immediately turned around and went back to work at the high school. The students were glad to have their Kimo back. They had deemed first one substitute teacher and then another simply not up to their standards.

A scant two months later, on May 19, 1982, all eighteen students from Jaime's calculus class powered through the challenging AP exam. The test consisted of forty-five multiple choice questions and seven free-response problems. The students were confident about their answers to the multiple choice questions and were able to work their way through most of the word problems on the free response section. Question number 6, however, was perplexing. Reaching the correct answer required the ability to calculate the cost of a tank 4 meters wide and with a volume of 36 cubic meters, constructed with a rectangular base, 4 rectangular sides, and an open top. The formula for calculating the correct response to a problem like this would have been covered during the time that Jaime suffered his heart attack. One of Jaime's substitutes had offered a formula for volume problems, which some of the test takers vaguely remembered, and they attempted to use that formula to work the problem. Others, knowing this material had not been covered, simply moved on to the other questions, believing that if they did well enough on the other portions of the test, they could still earn a passing score (Mathews 1988, 144).

When they received their test results, all eighteen students were exuberant when they were informed that they had passed. However, two months later, fourteen of the students received letters from the Educational Testing Service (ETS) in Princeton, New Jersey, stating that their scores were invalidated. The ETS suspected the Garfield students had cheated because several of them had made similar errors, errors that were unusual, on their exams. What put the ETS scorers on high alert was the repetition of an incorrect formula used to attempt a solution to question number 6 (Mathews 1988, 147). The students' initial exuberance turned to disbelief, then to indignation, and then to fuming anger.

Jaime, too, was at first incredulous and then incensed. He believed the students' passing scores had been challenged because they were earned by Hispanic students from a poor high school, and that the ETS couldn't believe such students were capable of scoring well on such an advanced test. The maligned students were vindicated, however, when twelve of the fourteen agreed, grudgingly, to retake the test, and they all passed with flying colors. The 1988 movie *Stand and Deliver* chronicled these events. Following the release of this inspirational movie, President Ronald Reagan hailed Jaime Escalante as a hero on national television. In the spring of 1988, Jaime was seated in the audience as seven of the twelve students from his 1982 class graduated from the engineering program at the prestigious University of Southern California.

In 1991, Jaime and Fabiola desired a change of scenery and decided to move to northern California. Jaime was hired to teach math at Hiram W. Johnson High School in the Sacramento City Unified School District. That same year, he developed a Peabody Award-winning public television series called *Futures*, which explored ways in which math is used in every day life, and additional topics about math, science, and careers (Morey and Dunn 1996, 25).

"I exhibit deep love and caring for my students," Jaime once said. "I have no exclusive claim to these attributes; they are as natural as breathing to most parents and teachers. The power of love and concern in changing young lives should not be overlooked" (Escalante and Dirmann 1990). In recognition of Jaime Escalante's outstanding contributions in the field of education, he received the White House Hispanic Heritage Award in 1989, and in 1990, he was given the Jefferson Award from the American Institute for Public Service. In 1998, Jaime earned the Free Spirit Award from the Freedom Forum, the Andres Bello Prize from the Organization of American States, and the United States Presidential

Medal for Excellence. The following year, Jaime was inducted into the National Teachers Hall of Fame.

After teaching in Sacramento for seven years, Jaime retired in 1998 at the age of sixty-seven. Following his retirement, Jaime and Fabiola returned to their native country of Bolivia, after an absence of thirty-five years. They settled in her hometown of Cochabamba, approximately 230 miles east of La Paz. Jaime became a part-time math professor at the Universidad del Valle, where he continued to teach calculus until 2008. But he frequently returned to the United States to fulfill engagements as a motivational speaker and to work as an educational consultant for both President George W. Bush and California Governor Arnold Schwarzenegger.

Jaime Escalante succumbed to bladder cancer on March 30, 2010, in Roseville, California, at the home of his older son, Jaime, Jr. He was seventy-nine years old. He was buried at Rose Hills Memorial Park in Whittier, California. In his *Los Angeles Times* obituary, Gaston Caperton, the former governor of West Virginia and President of the College Board, expressed his high praise for the long-time educator. "Jaime Escalante has left a deep and enduring legacy in the struggle for academic equity in American education. His passionate belief (was) that all students, when properly prepared and motivated, can succeed at academically demanding course work, no matter what their racial, social, or economic background."

The teaching goes on ...
MITCH ALBOM

Glossary

accommodation school: an alternative school regulated and maintained by a county superintendent, as opposed to a traditional school district. Typically, these schools fall into three categories: those that are similar to traditional schools, alternative schools, and schools located in juvenile detention centers.

advanced placement: college level courses offered to high school students who, upon successful completion, earn college credits.

boarding school: a school where the students not only receive an education, but where they also receive room and board.

Chiefs' Children's School: a private school established in the Hawaiian Islands for the purpose of providing an education in Western ways of life to the royal children of Native Hawaiian kings and chiefs.

college preparatory school: a school which provides curriculum designed to prepare students for the rigors of college courses.

community-centered education: a progressive instructional program designed by New York City teacher Leonard Covello that was characterized by a close working relationship between the school and the community. Students participated in social-service programs, recreational pursuits, and cultural activities, and members of the community were actively involved with programs that took place at the school.

community school: a publicly funded institution that serves both as a school and as a community center, providing family support, health and social services, and other resources before, during, and after the school day, and on the weekends.

day school: a school where the students attend classes during the day, but return to their parents' homes each evening.

emancipation school: literacy schools that were organized by the Union during the Civil War to provide an education for the children of escaped and newly emancipated slaves.

Farm Cadet Bureau: during World War I, an employment program for high school students sponsored by the Committee on War Service and organized by the board of education in Milton, New York. The Bureau trained students to work in the state's fruit and berry industry to fill a critical shortage of manual labor that resulted from so many farm workers enlisting in the war.

farm school: a boarding school, which primarily served young boys, that provided training in agricultural skills and fundamental literacy skills in such subjects as reading, writing, and mathematics. Also, the facility provided for the students' housing, food, and medical care. The purpose of the farm school was to offer orphan or homeless boys the opportunity to learn a marketable skill, which would enable them to find employment on farms in the Midwest or the South.

Freedmen's Bureau: a federal agency established by President

Abraham Lincoln during the Reconstruction period, 1865–1869, which provided assistance to freed slaves in the form of housing, food, health care, education, and jobs.

freedom school: a school that was established to provide instruction to African American students who had been denied a basic education because of discrimination. Typically, freedom schools offered a curriculum that strengthened basic literacy skills such as reading, writing, mathematics, and verbal skills. Additionally, lesson plans emphasized knowledge of the Constitution, African American history, leadership development, and current events, including the most recent developments in the civil rights movement of the 1960s.

ganas: a Spanish-language term meaning the desire to learn, the ability to sacrifice, the wish to get ahead.

Harlem Renaissance: a cultural movement promoting the development of African American literature, music, and art which spanned the 1920s and 1930s.

homeschool: the practice of educating children at home, most often by the parents, but sometimes with tutors, rather than in other more formal settings, such as a public or private school.

Indian boarding school: a boarding school where Native American students were sent, sometimes involuntarily, for the purpose of educating them and preparing them for assimilation into the culture of the white majority.

industrial school: a boarding school that provided for the children's basic needs for housing, food, and medical care. Students were taught vocational skills, which would allow them to seek gainful employment. For example, girls received training in the domestic arts or needle crafts, and boys were taught vocational skills such as carpentry, shoe-making, or box-making. In addition, the young people were taught fundamental literacy skills in such subjects that included reading, writing, and mathematics.

Japanese language school: a school organized by Japanese parents who were concerned about the increasing Americanization of their American-born children. The curriculum stressed Japanese language, culture, and customs.

Kamehameha Schools: private schools, one for boys and one for girls, established in the state of Hawaii by the Bernice Pauahi Bishop Charitable Trust for the purpose of providing educational opportunities for Native Hawaiians.

normal school: a school which provided training for high school graduates who wished to become teachers. Training included courses in subjects that teachers would be expected to teach to their students, and instruction on how to organize and present lessons.

Orphan Train: a train that carried small groups of orphans from East Coast cities such as New York, to farming communities in the Midwest or South for the purpose of finding adoptive homes for the children. The practice was discontinued by about 1930.

probationary school: a secondary school established to provide education for juvenile delinquents and students with discipline and attendance issues.

relocation camp school: a school set up in an internment camp for Japanese Americans during World War II.

reservation day school: a school located on an Indian reservation where Native American students attended classes during the day, but returned to their parents' tribal homes each evening.

segregation academy: a series of private schools for white students that were established in Prince Edward County, Virginia, and funded by state money and tax credits from the county as a way of avoiding integration ordered by the Supreme Court in their decision of *Brown vs. Board of Education.*

settlement house: an organization established in an impoverished neighborhood which offers food, shelter, citizenship classes, and educational opportunities to the community. A settlement house is typically financed by charitable donations contributed by wealthy sponsors and staffed by volunteers.

soup school: a school that provides assistance to immigrant populations about how to assimilate within the dominant culture. The main curriculum of soup schools was instruction on the English language, basic literacy skills, and American culture. The facility derives its name from the daily distribution of a bowl of nourishing soup to each student.

specialist school: a secondary school which specializes in a particular curriculum for the purpose of boosting achievement in that specific subject or skill.

Underground Railroad: a secret route of safe houses created in the 1830s to assist runaway slaves in their journey out of slavery in the South to freedom in the North. Escaped slaves often walked long distances and usually traveled at night to stay out of sight, and, if caught, they were returned to their owners where they often suffered severe punishments for their escape attempts.

Bibliography

Chapter 1: Charlotte Forten Grimke

Bolden, Tonya. 1988. *And Not Afraid to Dare: The Stories of Ten African American Women.* New York: Scholastic Press.

Boyd, Herb, ed. 2000. *Autobiography of a People: Three Centuries of African American History Told by Those Who Lived It.* New York: Doubleday.

Burchard, Peter. 1995. *Charlotte Forten: A Black Teacher in the Civil War.* New York: Crown Publishers, Inc.

Forten, Charlotte. 1864. "Life on the Sea Islands, Part I." *Atlantic Monthly* XIII (May): 587–596.

Forten, Charlotte. 1864. "Life on the Sea Islands, Part II." *Atlantic Monthly* XIII (June): 666–676.

Grimke, Charlotte Forten. 1988. *The Journals of Charlotte Forten Grimke.* Edited by Brenda Stevenson. New York: Oxford University Press, Inc.

Smith, Jessie Carney, and Linda T. Wynn. 2009. *Freedom Facts and Firsts: 400 Years of the African American Civil Rights Experience.* Canton, Michigan: Visible Ink Press.

Chapter 2: Elaine Goodale Eastman

Benbow-Pfalzgraf, Taryn, ed. 2000. *American Women Writers: A Critical Reference Guide from Colonial Times to Present, 2nd ed.* Vol. 2: 5-6. Detroit, Michigan: St. James Press.

BIBLIOGRAPHY

Brown, Dee. *Bury My Heart at Wounded Knee: An Indian History of the American West.* 1970. New York: Henry Holt and Company.

Cassidy, James J., Jr., ed. 1995. *Through Indian Eyes.* Pleasantville, New York: Reader's Digest Association, Inc.

Churchill, Ward. 2004. *Kill the Indian, Save the Man: The Genocidal Impact of American Indian Residential Schools.* San Francisco, California: City Light Books.

Cooper, Michael L. 1999. *Indian School: Teaching the White Man's Way.* New York: Clarion Books.

DiSilvestro, Roger L. 2005. *In the Shadow of Wounded Knee: The Untold Final Story of the Indian Wars.* New York: Walker & Company.

Eastman, Elaine Goodale. 1900. "A New Method of Indian Education." *The Outlook* (Jan. 27) Vol. 64, No. 4: 222–224.

Eastman, Elaine Goodale. 1935. *Pratt: The Red Man's Moses.* Norman, Oklahoma: University of Oklahoma Press.

Eastman, Elaine Goodale. 1978. *Sister to the Sioux: The Memoirs of Elaine Goodale Eastman 1885-1891.* Edited by Kay Graber. Lincoln, Nebraska: University of Nebraska Press.

Easton, John, Commissioner. 1880. "The Indian School at Carlisle Barracks." (Aug. 9) Washington, D C: Department of the Interior Bureau of Education.

Sargent, Theodore D. 2005. *The Life of Elaine Goodale Eastman.* Lincoln, Nebraska: University of Nebraska Press.

CHAPTER 3: JULIA RICHMAN

Berrol, Selma Cantor. 1995. *Growing Up American: Immigrant Children in America, Then and Now.* New York: Twayne Publishers.

Berrol, Selma Cantor. 2009. "Julia Richman." *Jewish Women: A Comprehensive Historical Encyclopedia.* http://jwa.org/encyclopedia/article/richman_julia.

Berrol, Selma Cantor. 1993. *Julia Richman: A Notable Woman.* Philadelphia, Pennsylvania: The Balch Institute Press.

Brody, Seymour Sy. 1996. *Jewish Heroes and Heroines of America: 150 True*

Stories of American Jewish Heroism. Hollywood, Florida: Lifetime Books, Inc.

Commire, Anne, ed. 2001. "Richman, Julia." *Women in World History: A Biographical Encyclopedia* Vol. 13, 285. Detroit, Michigan: The Gale Group.

Encyclopedia.com. 2001. "Julia Richman 1855-1912." http://www.encyclopedia.com.

Public Broadcasting System, PBS Online. n.d. "Schoolhouse Pioneers: Julia Richman." http://www.pbs.org/onlyateacher/richman.html.

Richman, Julia, and Isabel Richman Wallach. 1908. *Good Citizenship.* New York: American Book Co.

Sternlicht, Sanford. 2004. *The Tenement Saga: The Lower East Side and Early Jewish American Writers.* Madison, Wisconsin: University of Wisconsin Press.

Von Drehle, David. 2003. *Triangle: The Fire That Changed America.* New York: Atlantic Monthly Press.

Watson, Milton H. 1987. *Disasters at Sea.* Wellingborough, Northamptonshire: Thorsons Publishing Group.

CHAPTER 4: ANNE SULLIVAN MACY

Braddy, Nella. 1993. *Anne Sullivan Macy: The Story Behind Helen Keller.* Garden City, New York: Doubleday, Doran & Company, Inc.

Keller, Helen. 1957. *Teacher Anne Sullivan Macy: A Tribute by the Foster-Child of Her Mind.* Garden City, New York: Delacorte Press.

Keller, Helen. 1988. *The Story of My Life.* New York: Bantam Books.

Lash, Joseph P. 1980. *Helen and Teacher: The Story of Helen Keller and Anne Sullivan Macy.* New York: Delacorte Press.

Lawlor, Laurie. 2001. *Helen Keller: Rebellious Spirit.* New York: Holiday House.

Nielsen, Kim E. 2009. *Beyond the Miracle Worker: The Remarkable Life of Anne Sullivan Macy and Her Extraordinary Friendship with Helen Keller.* Boston, Massachusetts: Beacon Press.

Taylor, Jean Welt. 2004. *Gentle Hand to Victory: The Life of Annie Sullivan (Helen Keller's Teacher)*. Bloomington, Indiana: XLibris.

CHAPTER 5: CARTER GODWIN WOODSON

Bennett, Lerone, Jr. 2005. "Carter G. Woodson, Father of Black History: A Profile of the Founder of Black History Month." Reprinted by permission from Ebony. Johnson Publishing Co. http://www.america.gov/st/diversity-english.

Branham, Charles R., PhD. 1998. *Profiles of Great African Americans*. Lincolnwood, Illinois: Publications International, Ltd.

Dagbovie, Pero Gaglo. 2007. *The Early Black History Movement: Carter G. Woodson and Lorenzo Johnston Greene*. Chicago, Illinois: University of Illinois Press.

Encyclopedia of World Biography. 1998. "Carter Woodson." Vol. 26: 374-376. Detroit, Michigan: The Gale Group.

Gates, Henry Louis, Jr., and Cornel West. 2000. *The African American Century: How Black Americans Have Shaped Our Country*. New York: Touchstone.

Goggin, Jacqueline. 1993. *Carter G. Woodson: A Life in Black History*. Baton Rouge, Louisiana: Louisiana State University Press.

Greene, Lorenzo J. 1996. *Selling Black History for Carter G. Woodson: A Diary, 1930–1933*. Ed. by Arvarh E. Strickland. Columbia, Missouri: University of Missouri Press.

Palmer, Colin A., ed. 2005. "Carter Woodson." *Encyclopedia of African American Culture and History* Vol. 5, 2332-2333. Detroit, Michigan: The Gale Group.

Pyne, Charlynn Spencer. 1994. "The Burgeoning Cause, 1920–1930: An Essay on Carter G. Woodson." http://www.loc.gov/loc/lcib/94/9403/woodson.html.

CHAPTER 6: CLARA COMSTOCK

Bernstein, Nina. 2001. *The Lost Children of Wilder: The Epic Struggle to Change Foster Care*. New York: Pantheon Books.

Call, Richard H. 1999. "My Story and What I Remember of My Parents and Miss Clara Comstock." *The Crooked Lake Review.* Issue #111 (Spring). http://www.crookedlakereview.com.

Comstock, Clara. 1957. Speech delivered to the Children's Aid Society, New York. (Nov. 20, 1957).

Fry, Annette R. 1994. *The Orphan Trains.* New York: New Discovery Books.

Holt, Marilyn Irvin. 1992. *The Orphan Trains: Placing Out in America.* Lincoln, Nebraska: University of Nebraska Press.

Melosh, Barbara. 2001. *Strangers and Kin: The American Way of Adoption.* Cambridge, Massachusetts: Harvard University Press.

National Orphan Train Complex Museum and Research Center. n.d. www.orphantraindepot.com.

O'Connor, Stephen. 2001. *Orphan Trains: The Story of Charles Loring Brace and the Children He Saved and Failed.* Boston, Massachusetts: Houghton Mifflin Company.

Warren, Andrea. 1996. *Orphan Train Rider: One Boy's True Story.* Boston, Massachusetts: Houghton Mifflin Company.

Warren, Andrea. 2001. *We Rode the Orphan Trains.* Boston, Massachusetts: Houghton Mifflin Company.

CHAPTER 7: EULALIA BOURNE

Arizona Humanities Council. 2009. "School on the Range: The Little Cowpuncher Roundup." http://www.parentseyes.arizona.edu/LC2/sister1/html.

Bourne, Eulalia. 1969. *Nine Months is a Year at Baboquivari School.* Tucson, Arizona: University of Arizona Press.

Bourne, Eulalia. 1974. *Ranch Schoolteacher.* Tucson, Arizona: University of Arizona Press.

Bourne, Eulalia, ed. 1932-1942. *Little Cowpuncher.* Tucson, Arizona: University of Arizona. http://cowpuncher.library.arizon.edu.

Bourne, Eulalia. 1967. *Woman in Levi's.* Tucson, Arizona: University of

Arizona Press. Online version. http://www.uapress.arizona.
edu/onlinebks.

Hayes, Allan, and Carol Hayes. 2006. *The Desert Southwest: Four Thousand Years of Life and Art*. Berkley, California: Ten Speed Press.

Seagraves, Anne. 1996. *Daughters of the West*. Hayden, Idaho: Wesanne Publications.

CHAPTER 8: LEONARD COVELLO

Berrol, Selma Cantor. 1995. *Growing Up American: Immigrant Children in America, Then and Now*. New York: Twayne Publishers.

Covello, Leonard, and Guido D'Agostino. 1958. *The Heart is the Teacher*. New York: McGraw Hill.

Johanek, Michael C., and John L. Puckett. 2007. *Leonard Covello and the Making of Benjamin Franklin High School: Education as if Citizenship Mattered*. Philadelphia, Pennsylvania: Temple University Press.

Meyer, Gerald, PhD. n.d. "The Cultural Pluralist Response to Americanization: Horace Kallen, Randolph Bourne, Louis Adamic, and Leonard Covello." *Journal of the Research Group on Socialism and Democracy* Vol. 22, No. 3. http://www.sdonline.org/48/the-cultual-pluralist-response-to-amiericanization.

Meyer, Gerald, PhD. n.d. "Leonard Covello: Cultural Pluralism." http://www.vitomarcantonio.com/lc_marcantonio_and_leo_covello_collaboration.html#.

Perrone, Vito. 1998. *Teacher with a Heart: Reflections on Leonard Covello and Community*. New York: Teachers College Press.

Weldon, Shawn. 1982. "Leonard Covello 1907-1974." The Research Library of the Balch Institute for Ethnic Studies. http://www2.hsp.org/collections/Balch.

CHAPTER 9: GLADYS KAMAKAKUOKALANI BRANDT

Apgar, Sally. "Famed and Respected Educator, Civic Leader and Mainstay in the Hawaiian Community, Dies." *Star Bulletin*.

Jan. 16, 2003. http://archives.starbulletin.com/2003/01/16/news/story1.html.

Apgar, Sally. "Farewell Auntie: Hawaiians Unite to Remember a Life of Public Service." *Star Bulletin.* Jan. 30, 2003, http://archives.starbulletin.com/2003/01/30/news/story1.html.

Brandt, Gladys Kamakakuokalani. 1986. Keynote address, delivered at Kamehameha School Centennial Staff Convocation in Honolulu, Hawaii.

Daws, Gavan. 1968. *Shoal of Time: A History of the Hawaiian Islands.* Honolulu, Hawaii: University of Hawaii Press.

Daws, Gavan, and Na Leo O. Kamehameha. 2009. *Wayfinding Through the Storm: Speaking Truth to Power at Kamehameha Schools 1993–1999.* Honolulu, Hawaii: Watermark Publishing.

Delta Kappa Gamma Society International. 1981. *Makers of Destiny, Hawaiian Style: The Lives of Pioneer Women Educators in Hawaii.* Honolulu, Hawaii: The Delta Kappa Gamma Society International.

Eyre, Kawika. 2004. "Suppression of Hawaiian Culture at Kamehameha Schools." http://apps.ksbe.edu/kaiwakiloumoku/makalii/feature-stories.

Ishikawa, Scott, and Beverly Creamer. "Gladys Brandt, Champion of Hawaiian Culture." *The Honolulu Advertiser.* Jan. 17, 2003. http://the/honolulu.advertiser.com/article/2003/Jan/17/In/In04a.html.

King, Samuel P., and Randall W. Roth. 2006. *Broken Trust: Greed, Mismanagement & Political Manipulation at America's Largest Charitable Trust.* Honolulu, Hawaii: University of Hawaii Press.

Rath, J. Arthur. 2006. *Lost Generations: A Boy, a School, a Princess.* Honolulu, Hawaii: University of Hawaii Press.

Roth, Randall W. "Politics in Hawaii: Is Something Broken?" *Honolulu Magazine.* May, 2008. http://www.honolulumagazine.com/Honolulu-Magazine/May-2008/Politics-in-Hawaii.

Williams, Waimea. 2004. *Aloha, Kauai: A Childhood*. Waipahu, Hawaii: Island Heritage Publishing.

CHAPTER 10: MARY TSUKAMOTO

AETN (Arkansas Educational Television Network). *WWII Oral History Project*. 2010. Arkansas: Arkansas Department of Education. http://www.intheirwords.org/the_home_front_experience/internment_camps.

Dudley, William, ed. 2002. *Japanese American Internment Camps*. San Diego, California: Greenhaven Press, Inc.

Go For Broke National Educational Center. n.d. www.goforbroke.org.

Grapes, Bryan J., ed. 2001. *Japanese American Internment Camps*. San Diego, California: Greenhaven Press, Inc.

Howard, John. 2008. *Concentration Camps on the Home Front: Japanese Americans in the House of Jim Crow*. Chicago, Illinois: The University of Chicago Press.

National Women's History Project. 2006. "2006 Honorees: Mary Tsukamoto." National Women's History Project. http://www.nwhp.org/whm/tsukamoto_bio.php.

Takemoto, Paul Howard. 2006. *Nisei Memories: My Parents Talk About the War Years*. Seattle, Washington: University of Washington Press.

Tateishi, John, ed. 1984. *And Justice for All: An Oral History of the Japanese American Detention Camps*. New York: Random House.

Tsukamoto, Mary, and Elizabeth Pinkerton. 1988. *We the People: A Story of Internment in America*. Elk Grove, California: Laguna Publishers.

CHAPTER 11: SANDRA ADICKES

Adickes, Sandra E. 2005. *The Legacy of a Freedom School*. New York: Palgrave MacMillan.

Adickes v. S.H. Kress & Co., 398 U.S. 144, 90 S. Ct. 1598, 26 L. Ed., 2n 142, 1970. U.S. 31.

Aretha, David. 2008. *The Civil Rights Movement: Freedom Summer*. Greensboro, North Carolina: Morgan Reynolds Publishing.

Boyd, Herb. 2004. *We Shall Overcome*. Naperville, Illinois: Sourcebooks, Inc.

Branch, Taylor. 1998. *Pillar of Fire: America in the King Years 1963–1965*. New York: Simon & Schuster.

"Civil Rights Movement Veterans." 2012. www.crmvet.org.

Erenrich, Susie, ed. 1999. *Freedom Is a Constant Struggle: An Anthology of the Mississippi Civil Rights Movement*. Montgomery, Alabama: Black Belt Press.

Lewis, Andrew B. 2009. *The Shadows of Youth: The Remarkable Journey of the Civil Rights Generation*. New York: Hill and Want.

Virginia Historical Society. Richmond, Virginia. "Civil Rights." www. vahistorical.org.

Watson, Bruce. 2010. *Freedom Summer: The Savage Season That Made Mississippi Burn and Made America a Democracy*. New York: Viking.

CHAPTER 12: JAIME ESCALANTE

Byers, Ann. 1996. *Jaime Escalante: Sensational Teacher*. Berkeley Heights, New Jersey: Enslow Publishers, Inc.

Escalante, Jaime, and Jack Dirmann. 1990. "Jaime Escalante Math Program." *Journal of Negro Education* Vol. 59, No. 3 (Summer). http://www.thefutureschannel.com/jaime_escalante/jaime_escalante_math_program.php.

Mathews, Jay. 1988. *Escalante: The Best Teacher in America*. New York: Henry Holt and Company.

Morey, Janet Nomura, and Wendy Dunn. 1996. *Famous Hispanic Americans*. New York: Cobblehill Books.

Schraff, Anne. 2009. *Jaime Escalante: Inspirational Math Teacher*. Berkeley Heights, New Jersey: Enslow Publishers, Inc.

UXL Hispanic American Biography, 2nd Edition. 2003. Detroit, Michigan: The Gale Group, Inc. pgs. 87–88.

Woo, Elaine. "Jaime Escalante Dies at 79; Math Teacher Who Challenged East L.A. Students to 'Stand and Deliver.'" *Los Angeles Times*. March 31, 2010.

INDEX

ABOUT THE AUTHOR

Terry Lee Marzell has been an educator in Corona, California, for the past thirty-one years, working at both the high-school and the junior high-school levels. She has a bachelor's degree in English from California State University, Fullerton, and a master's in interdisciplinary studies from California State University, San Bernardino. In addition, she successfully completed the program for the Inland Area Writing Project. To develop her artistic side, Terry fulfilled the requirements for Level 1 coursework in interior design at Mount San Antonio Junior College in Walnut, California. She has taught English, developmental reading, journalism, drama, library science, geography, and interior design. Throughout her long career as an educator, she has worked with English-language learners and students in honors courses, and she has been a mentor for both International Baccalaureate candidates and special education students. She has also served as her school's teacher librarian. She lives in Chino Hills, California, with her husband, Hal.

CPSIA information can be obtained at www.ICGtesting.com
Printed in the USA
LVOW060113140912

298743LV00004B/18/P